MACBETH
High King of Scotland
1040–57

Peter Berresford Ellis

BARNES
&NOBLE
BOOKS
NEW YORK

DEDICATION

Do dheagh charaid
 Seumas Mac a' Ghobhainn
Le mór-mheas as leth na strì gun stad a rinn e, bàs mi-nàdurra na
Gàidhlig a bhacadh – a cànain a bha aig aon àm 'na cànain
choitcheann o cheann gu ceann Alba.

'S i labhair Alba,
'S Gall-bhodacha féin;
Ar flaith, ar prionnsai,
 'S ar diùcanna gun éis
An tigh-comhairl' an righ,
'Nuair shuidheadh air bìnn
a' chùirt.

Alasdair Mac Mhaighstir Alasdair, 1751.

This edition published by Barnes & Noble, Inc.,
by arrangement with A. M. Heath & Co. Ltd.

1993 Barnes & Noble Books

ISBN 1-56619-299-4
Printed and bound in the United States of America

M 9 8 7 6 5 4 3 2 1

CONTENTS

THE SPELLING OF MACBETH'S NAME

I have adopted the anglicized spelling, MacBeth, but reasserted a capital 'B', which Shakespeare puts in lower case (*viz* Macbeth), as a more common way of rendering the Scottish Gaelic name Mac Bheatha into English phonetics.

The word *Mac*, as in all Goidelic Celtic languages (Irish, Manx and Scottish), means 'son' and is usually prefixed to a father's name which has evolved over the years into a standard surname; i.e. Mac Lean, Mac Innes, Mac Cormick, Mac Donald and so forth. As the names became more anglicized, there has been a tendency to run them together, sometimes dropping the capital letter of the actual name, hence Maclean, Macdonald etc. In other cases there has also been a tendency to shorten the word *Mac* into *Mc* such as McAdam or McKinlay.

Where I refer specifically to Shakespeare's character I bow to his rendering of Macbeth.

INTRODUCTION

The popular image of MacBeth, High King of Scotland from AD 1040 to 1057, is the 'Macbeth' of the Shakespearian drama – an ambitious, power-crazed man, treacherous and evil to a psychopathic degree, spurred on by his fiendish wife to one act of barbarism after another.

The popularity of *Macbeth* has made it one of the most widely translated of Shakespeare's plays, not only into other languages but into other media. *Macbeth* has been the subject of a grand opera by Giuseppe Verdi (1847), a symphonic poem by Richard Strauss (1887), and a number of minor works ranging from Purcell to Lawrence Collingwood's 1934 operatic version.

The play has been successfully adapted for the screen by a number of film directors, including George Schaefer and Roman Polanski. Not only have film directors been content to adapt the Shakespearian drama as Shakespeare wrote it but some have translated the 'eternal story' to different historical epochs and different cultural settings – such as the production of *Joe Macbeth* (1955), which turned the Scottish ruler into a Chicago hoodlum engaged in a gangland power struggle, and *Throne of Blood* (1957), a Japanese version in which Macbeth appears as Washizu, a medieval Japanese kinglet.

MacBeth is possibly the most universally known of Scottish monarchs but he is known only by his Shakespearian colouring. What of the historical MacBeth? According to Clayton Hutton (*Macbeth: The Making of the Film*, 1960):

If it hadn't been for the inspired dramatic craftsmanship of William Shakespeare, slapping down the vivid lines of his new drama with his headlong goose-feather pen, Macbeth today would be merely a crazed little murdering kinglet, dead these nine hundred years – and forgotten almost entirely.

Yet, on the other hand, according to John MacBeth (*MacBeth, King, Queen and Clan*, 1921):

King MacBeth is one of the greater figures appearing on the horizon of Scottish history. His actions as king, soldier, general and patriot won him distinction in his day. Unfortunately for his fair name the later romances laid the crimes of others to his charge so that now he stands before the world branded with 'every sin that has a name'.

It is, of course, impossible to dispute with Clayton Hutton that, had it not been for Shakespeare, MacBeth would have been 'forgotten almost entirely' today. But that forgetfulness would have occurred not for the reasons which Clayton Hutton assumes. Between the age of MacBeth and the Scotland of today there is the deep abyss of a forgotten culture and a nearly dead language. Through the vagaries of translation, distortion and pure invention, the MacBeth who ruled Scotland wisely and well for seventeen years has come down to us through a glass darkly as the 'devilish Macbeth'.

However, there are enough contemporary sources by which to rescue the good name of the historical MacBeth and that is the intention of this work: to present the real MacBeth for judgement – while, at the same time, not slighting the greatness of William Shakespeare's creation. If Shakespeare's Macbeth is false, it is not because Shakespeare wished it so or even knew it to be so. In writing his play he used the best historical sources available in the English language in the London of his day. The result was one of the great masterpieces of literature.

But to talk of Shakespeare's Macbeth as the MacBeth of historical reality is, indeed, to malign a ruler who stands head and shoulders above the feuds and petty squabbles which ravaged the kingdoms of Europe in the eleventh century. It is ironic that MacBeth and Scotland were singled out by Shakespeare when the contemporary dynastic struggles in England were, by comparison, far more murderous. While rulers came and went in neighbouring England, Norway and Denmark, MacBeth ruled in security and peace in Scotland. At no time during MacBeth's kingship did a Scottish army march outside the borders of Scotland, and for the first fourteen years of his reign no envious monarch in England, Norway or Denmark felt strong enough to invade Scottish territory. MacBeth brought peace and security to Scotland. Elsewhere the great royal families of Europe demonstrated how efficiently they could kill, cheat and rob. One English monarch had his brother's eyes put out for attempting to claim the throne, another had his brother's body dug up and beheaded. Poisoners practised their skills freely, as brothers and cousins, even mothers and sons, turned on each other in a bloody scramble for power.

Against this background it was inevitable that MacBeth, bound as he was by his own particular social and cultural ethics, should fall to someone more ruthless than himself. This, then, is that story.

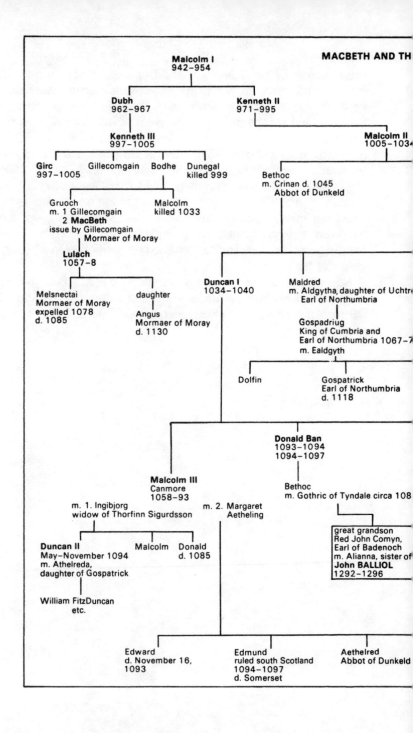

Malcolm I
942–954

Dubh
962–967

Kenneth II
971–995

Kenneth III
997–1005

Malcolm II
1005–103

Girc
997–1005

Gillecomgain

Bodhe

Dunegal
killed 999

Bethoc
m. Crinan d. 1045
Abbot of Dunkeld

Gruoch
m. 1 Gillecomgain
2 **MacBeth**
issue by Gillecomgain
Mormaer of Moray

Malcolm
killed 1033

Lulach
1057–8

Melsnectai
Mormaer of Moray
expelled 1078
d. 1085

daughter

Angus
Mormaer of Moray
d. 1130

Duncan I
1034–1040

Maldred
m. Aldgytha, daughter of Uchtr
Earl of Northumbria

Gospadriug
King of Cumbria and
Earl of Northumbria 1067–7
m. Ealdgyth

Dolfin

Gospatrick
Earl of Northumbria
d. 1118

Donald Ban
1093–1094
1094–1097

Bethoc
m. Gothric of Tyndale circa 108

Malcolm III
Canmore
1058–93

m. 1. Ingibjorg
widow of Thorfinn Sigurdsson

m. 2. Margaret
Aetheling

great grandson
Red John Comyn,
Earl of Badenoch
m. Alianna, sister of
John BALLIOL
1292–1296

Duncan II
May–November 1094
m. Athelreda,
daughter of Gospatrick

Malcolm

Donald
d. 1085

William FitzDuncan
etc.

Edward
d. November 16,
1093

Edmund
ruled south Scotland
1094–1097
d. Somerset

Aethelred
Abbot of Dunkeld

Kings of Scotland **David**

Doada
m. Findlaech Mac Ruaridh
Mormaer of Moray d. 1020

MACBETH
1040–1057
m. Gruoch

daughter
m. Sigurd Hlodversson d. 1014
Jarl of Orkney

Thorfinn
Jarl of Orkney d. 1057
m. Ingibjorg

Paul d. 1098
Jarl of Orkney

Erlend d. 1098
Jarl of Orkney
m. Thora

St. Magnus
Jarl of Orkney

daughter

Moddan
d. 1040

Frakkok

Steinvar

Waltheof
Abbot of Dunkeld

Athelreda
m. **Duncan II**

Audhild

Eric Stakvallr
m. Ingigert

Melmore
m. Margaret, daughter of Haakron, Jarl of Orkney

Madach

Harald, Earl of Orkney circa 1180
m. 1. Afreca
2. Gormlath, daughter of Malcolm Macbeth

David
Jarl of Orkney
d. 1248

John
Jarl of Orkney
d. 1231

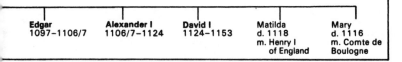

Edgar
1097–1106/7

Alexander I
1106/7–1124

David I
1124–1153

Matilda
d. 1118
m. Henry I
of England

Mary
d. 1116
m. Comte de
Boulogne

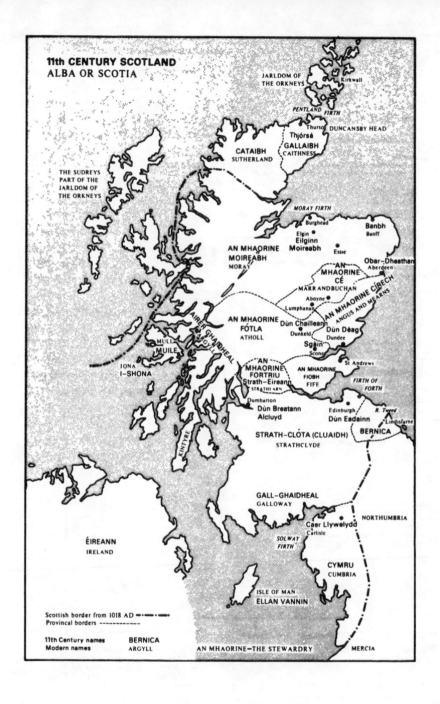

CHAPTER ONE

'They elected a king alternatively'
Clayton Hutton

Late in August, 1040, the citizens of Scone, the capital of Scotland, gathered in the streets of the royal city to watch the entry of a victorious army. It was an army of clansmen from Moray, the country's most northerly province. A few weeks before, on 14 August, these men with their Norse allies from the Orkneys, had met the army of the High King of Scotland, which was made up mostly of clansmen from Atholl and the south of the country, together with a contingent of Irish mercenaries, and defeated it near Burghead. In the course of the battle the thirty-nine-year-old High King, Duncan Mac Crinan, had been slain.

It would be wrong to assume that the citizens of Scone were unduly sorrowful at the death of the High King. He had not been a popular monarch and his greed and territorial ambition had led to civil war and his subsequent downfall. During his five-year reign Duncan had led his Scottish clans into five battles, each part of an unpopular expansionist war, and had been five times defeated. Therefore the citizens of Scone looked upon the Moray clansmen not so much as rebels or conquerors but as liberators who had deposed a tyrannical ruler.

The victorious thirty-five-year-old commander who marched at the head of the clansmen was a tall man, with red hair and a ruddy complexion. He was the Mormaer, or High Steward, of the northern province of Moray, the son of a previous Mormaer and grandson of Malcolm II (1005–34), who had been High King

1

before Duncan. His name was MacBeth Mac Findlaech and, following Duncan's defeat and death, he had come to Scone to argue his case before the chieftains, churchmen and lawmakers of Scotland. He asserted that the House of Moray had as great a right, under the Celtic legal system, to the High Kingship of Scotland as the House of Atholl from which Duncan's claim derived.

MacBeth Mac Findlaech was destined to be one of the most famous of all the kings of Scotland.

MacBeth was born in 1005, so the ancient chroniclers inform us. He was the son of Findlaech Mac Ruaridh, the Mormaer of Moray, and of Doada, one of the daughters of Malcolm II, High King of Scotland. Scotland then was quite different from the Scotland of today. Only during MacBeth's childhood did the kingdom begin to be called Scotia, from which Latin name Scotland is derived, the word developing from the Irish 'scotti' or 'skirmishers' who began to settle along the western seaboard of the country early in the third century. The country in which MacBeth was born was called Alba, by which name it is still known in modern Scottish Gaelic.

The boundaries of the country differed greatly from the boundaries of modern-day Scotland. To the north and to the west the territories of the Orkney Islands, with Caithness and Sutherland on the mainland, and the Hebridean Islands, formed no part of the Scottish kingdom, although, from time to time, the kings of both Scotland and Norway tried to exert their influence over the fiercely independent jarls (earls) of the Orkneys. These jarls were Viking chiefs who spent their summers raiding and looting the islands.

The people of the Orkneys were Norse in speech and culture as were their settlements in Caithness and Sutherland, though here the Norse settlers tended to intermarry with the native Gaels. Similarly, the Norse settlements in the Hebrides were also quickly gaelicized through intermarriage. The Orkneys were finally annexed to Scotland by James III in 1471, while the Hebrides were ceded to Scotland in the thirteenth century, although they retained a great degree of independence until the seventeenth century. MacBeth's Scotland, therefore, had its northern border south of

Caithness and Sutherland, while the southern border stretched as far as the Lancashire border, almost to Barrow-in-Furness, the territory of Cumbria then being an integral part of Scotland.

The entire population of Scotland at this time was Celtic in speech and culture. North of the Rivers Clyde and Forth the people spoke the Goidelic or Gaelic form of Celtic which has survived to modern times in Scottish Gaelic, Irish and Manx. To the south, however, they spoke a different form of Celtic called Brythonic, the ancestor of Welsh, Breton and Cornish. However, apart from Cumbria, the Brythonic Celtic territories of southern Scotland were being rapidly absorbed into the main body of Gaelic-speaking Scotland. During the eleventh century, soon after MacBeth's death, the area became monolingual in Gaelic and most of the Brythonic place-names were gaelicized. MacBeth's Scotland was, therefore, Celtic in culture, and the Gaelic branch of Celtic was the *lingua franca* of the entire country − the language of the royal court, of administration, of law, of literature and even of religious worship.

Eleventh-century Scotland was ruled by an *Ard-Righ*, a High King, from his capital at Sgàin, or Scone, in present-day Perthshire. But the power in the kingdom was decentralized and the territories were divided into several administrative units. North of the Forth and Clyde there were six provinces which had been carved out of a territorial union of the Picts and Scots in the ninth century. The Picts were the earliest Celtic inhabitants of Scotland, so called from the Latin *Picti* or 'painted people'. For many years it was thought that the Picts constituted a separate nationality to the Celts, then that they were a Brythonic branch. Modern scholarship now favours the theory that the Picts were Gaelic in speech. All scholars agree that Gaelic was the common language of the Picts as far back as scholastic research can penetrate. A people also called Picts are recorded as dwelling in mid- and northern Ireland for many centuries; the last reference to these Irish Picts occurs in the *Annals of Ulster* in AD 809. In Scotland the Latin-named Pictavia was called Cruithne-tuath by the Picts themselves. Cruithne-tuath meant the tribal lands of Cruithne, the semi-mythical warrior who was said to have founded the Pictish monarchy.

The third century saw the last migrations to Scotland of Celts from Ireland – the Hiberni, Attecotti and the Scotti, as the Romans named them. The Brythonic-speaking Celts called them Gwyddell, hence the mutation into 'Goidel' and 'Gael'. Of the names given to these immigrants it was the name Scotti which became the most popular and by which the entire country has become known in modern times. These Scotti landed on the Argyll seaboard and called their new land Dalriada after their leader Cairbre Riada, son of Conaire II, King of Munster who had been driven north by a famine. Cairbre first established a new settlement in County Antrim in the north of Ireland, but he and his followers quarrelled and some settlers crossed the sea to Argyll and established a kingdom there. It was a descendant of the Dalriadans, Kenneth Mac Alpin, who, in 843, united the Dalriadan kingdom with the Pictish kingdoms of Cruithne-tuath and established the capital at Scone.

This united territory was divided into six provinces. Andrew, the Bishop of Caithness (d. 1184) counted seven provinces, but he included Cat (Caithness) which was, in MacBeth's time, part of the jarldom of Orkney. Explaining how this division came about, an anonymous Irish scribe writes: 'Seven of Cruithne's children divided Alba into seven divisions; the portion of Cat, of Cé, of Círech; the portions of Fiobh, of Moireabh and of Fótla, and of Fortriu. And it is the name of each man of them that is his own land.'

The six provinces were each known, for administrative purposes, as *An Mhaorine* – 'the stewardry'. This designation survives in one instance today in the anglicized form of Mearns. Each province was governed by a *mór-mhaor*, anglicized as a mormaer, a High Steward who was answerable only to the High King. The two biggest provinces were Moireabh (Moray) and Fótla (Atholl) and it was the power struggle between the mormaers of these two provinces which was to shape MacBeth's destiny.

The province of Moray, where MacBeth's father, Findlaech, ruled, was much larger than the present-day county of the same name. It stretched right across Scotland from the east coast of modern Aberdeenshire to the west coast which was often styled in official documents of later years: '*Ergadia quae ad Moravium pertinent*' – 'the parts of Argyll which pertain to Moray'. The

4

name Moireabh meant 'the seaboard settlement'. Significantly, the contemporary chroniclers refer to the Mormaers of Moray as *Righ na h-Alba*, Kings of Scotland. While this title cannot be taken literally, it is an indication that the House of Moray was regarded as having a just claim to the High Kingship of Scotland and that claim was to play an important part in the life of MacBeth. Geographically, Moray was the biggest of the Scottish provinces.

The second biggest province was that of Fótla or Atholl. This province was referred to in the ninth century *Book of Deer* as Athfhótla, hence its anglicization into Atholl. The name means 'new Ireland' and was probably given by the Dalriadans, whose kingdom covered the province which stretched from Scone in the east to the Mull of Kintyre in the west and also included the islands of Arran, Jura, Islay, Mull and the sacred island of Iona. It was from the Mormaers of Atholl, because they were descendants of the unifying Dalriadan rulers, that the High Kings of Scotland were usually chosen. Hence there was no love lost between the Houses of Moray and Atholl.

As well as the provinces of Moray and Atholl, there was the province of Círech, the territory of Angus and Mearns; the province of Cé, modern Marr and Buchan; the province of Fiobh, easily recognizable as modern Fife; and the province of Fortriu or Fortrenn, synonyms for Ireland, which covered Strathearn, bridging the Firth of Clyde and the Firth of Forth. Strathearn is a valley around Loch Earn, originally Loch Éireann or the Lake of Ireland.

The territories south of the Clyde and Forth, governed from Scone, had a different territorial standing to the northern provinces. They were not governed by mormaers but by petty kings under the suzerainty of the High King. They comprised two major Brythonic Celtic territories. The first was the kingdom of Clóta or Strathclyde, with its capital at Alcluyd, which eventually became known by the Gaelic name Dùn Breatann (Dumbarton) or 'the fortress of the Brythons'. This Strathclyde kingdom came under the rule of Scone during the reign of Constantine MacBeth (900–942).

The second Brythonic Celtic kingdom lay south of the Solway Firth and stretched down the west coast to just above Barrow-in-Furness. Its inhabitants called it Cymru, the name the Celts of

Wales call their country to this day. The English settlers retained
the Celtic name Cymru – pronounced Cumree – and anglicized it
to Cumbria. The kingdom was strategically protected from the
Angles on its eastern flank by the Cumbrian Mountains and the
capital of the kingdom lay at Caer Lliwelydd (Carlisle). Cumbria
was eventually conquered by Edmund of England who gave it to
Malcolm I of Scotland (943–954) as a bribe to enlist his military
aid. Cumbria remained the southernmost province of Scotland
until the late eleventh century by which time the individual
Brythonic Celtic language of the area had almost died out in the
face of pressure from English. At the time of MacBeth's birth
both Brythonic kingdoms seem to have been united under a petty
king named Owain Mac Domhnull.

It is fascinating to recall that the earliest poetry in what we now
call Welsh was written in the Scottish lowlands near Edinburgh.
Edinburgh was a Brythonic Celtic township called Dinas Eidyn.
The name was later gaelicized to Dùn Éadainn and then
anglicized to Edinburgh. It was Symeon of Durham who
miswrote the name as Edwinesburgh and started a popular legend
that the town was founded by Angles under a king named
Edwine.

Dinas Eidyn was, in fact, the capital of a Celtic tribe called the
Gododdin. One of the first 'Welsh' poems comes down to us in
Llyr Aneurin (*The Book of Aneurin*), a sixth-century poet living at
the court of Mynddawg Mwynvawr, king of the Gododdin at
Edinburgh. In the poem, *Y Gododdin*, Aneurin tells how 300
warriors of his people went to attack Caertraeth (Catterick,
Yorkshire) to try to reclaim it from the invading Angles. The
attack failed and the warriors were slain.

> Man in might, youth in years,
> Courage in battle.
> Swift, long-maned stallions
> Under the thigh of a fine lad.
> Behind him, on the lean, swift flank,
> His target, broad and bright,
> Swords blue and bright,
> And fringes of goldwork.
> There'll be not between us now
> Reproach or enmity –

Rather shall I make you
Songs in your praise.

Other famous 'Welsh' poets of the sixth century, such as Taliesin and Llywarch Hen, were actually born and brought up in lowland Scotland.

In the sixth century groups of Angles and Flemings began to settle around the mouth of the River Tweed and impose their rule on the native Brythonic Celts. They established a small kingdom which they called Bernica and which the Celts called Leudduniawn or Lothian. By the time MacBeth was born, this kingdom, with its ruling class of Angles and its peasant class of Celts, had become part of the earldom of Northumbria. (This 'Lothian' kingdom must not be confused with the modern day Lothian counties which were not so named until the last century.) The evidence is that the Angle-dominated area did not stretch much beyond the Lammermuir Hills.

This, then, was the national and geographic structure of MacBeth's Scotland. The main population was rural, organized into a fairly sophisticated tribal, or clan, society which subsisted mainly by means of pastoral and agricultural farming. Great areas of the land were mountainous and bleak, swept by cold northern winds, on which only root crops could be grown; in the more fertile and relatively sheltered areas of Strathclyde and Cumbria, crops such as wheat, barley and corn were grown. But most of the clans, even in the south, measured their wealth in terms of cattle herds, and cattle-raiding was a common pastime. The significance of cattle as a means of wealth has been emphasized many times in Celtic mythology. In the famous *Táin Bó Cúailnge* three-quarters of Ireland go to war with Ulster over the possession of a great bull.

The clans who dwelt on the coast or by loch shores were hardy fishermen and sailors. Sophisticated boat-building was essential if the vessels were to weather the stormy northern waters. Latin chroniclers more than once commented on the shipbuilding ability of the early Scots. Whether this maritime skill helped to promote a thriving Scottish trade with other parts of Europe is difficult to say; however, many Christian missionaries from Scotland travelled to Europe, so it may be assumed that some trading did take place. It must be remembered, though, that

Scottish sailors were under a tremendous disadvantage by being so near to the sea routes of the Vikings, who frequently swept down from their fjords to loot and sink any unsuspecting merchantmen.

Eleventh-century Scotland had not developed any large cities, as in England. The major part of the population lived in rural communities scattered throughout the country. There were many townships but these were often no more than a small collection of houses spread round some important *dùn* (fortress) which can be demonstrated from the number of modern Scottish towns and cities which still incorporate the Gaelic word *dùn* in the name. Other townships sprang up around churches and monastic settlements, which then became trading centres for merchants.

The laws which governed the kingdom were old and highly sophisticated. Although no specific codification of the Scottish Celtic legal system has survived, we have evidence that it was a close approximation to the Brehon Law system of Ireland, whose first known codification was in the fifth century. The name derives from the Gaelic word *breitheamh* – a judge. These laws are not unlike the Welsh law tracts of Hywel Dda and the Breton laws which were incorporated into the Treaty of Union with France in 1532, demonstrating that the system was common to all Celtic states.

The basis of society in MacBeth's day was the Celtic clan system which must not be confused with the inventions of the eighteenth and nineteenth centuries, with hereditary clan chiefs, feudal rights and obligations, and kilts bearing distinctive tartan patterns. This system was evolved for the better government of Scotland and to encourage Scots to enlist in the British army after the Scottish clans had been smashed at Culloden in 1746. The Scottish clan system of the eleventh century bore little resemblance to Sir Walter Scott's fanciful flights of imagination.

The country was governed by a wide range of chieftains, each clearly defined by law, from chieftains of minor clans to mormaers and petty kings, up to the High King himself. Under Celtic law all such offices were filled by election. The candidate was usually nominated by the current office holder when he felt the approach of death. The heir-elect was known as the tanist, from the Gaelic *tànaiste*, or second, and the system is generally known as tanistry. But mere nomination did not ensure succession. The candidate had to be approved by the tribal assembly or, in the case of mormaers and High Kings, by an assembly of clan chieftains and leading churchmen. The candidates for such elections obviously had to be capable of fulfilling the office and were therefore usually elected from particular families who had knowledge and experience of such duties. The feudal principle of primogeniture was not recognized in eleventh-century Scotland in regard to either rank or property. Instead, and in contrast to the hereditary right of inheritance practised by other nations, Celtic law provided for the election to every office with the admonition that the most worthy be elected.

Should a chieftain, even a High King, try to usurp the clansmen's authority, it was in their power to depose him and elect another ruler. He was limited and hemmed in by office and dependent on his clan (or on his chieftains in the case of a High King) so that it was usually easier for him to promote the welfare of his people and safer for him to conform to the intention of the law than to become either negligent or despotic.

This early democratic system was not without faults, however. While primogeniture was not recognized, there was an hereditary principle involved, in that candidates were usually chosen from particular families – which often led to feuds, as in the case of Moray and Atholl. The system also had a weakness in that rivals for office could agitate against an established ruler on the grounds of usurpation of office and, if they convinced a large enough section of the people, could throw the country into civil war. But that, of course, remains the weakness of modern democracy. Another weakness was brought to light when the system tried to exist alongside states which practised primogeniture and feudalism. An envious Celtic ruler, deposed by the electoral system, would often seek military help from neighbouring feudal monarchs, basing his action on the principle of primogeniture. Such issues gave Caesar an excuse to invade Britain and Henry II to invade Ireland, and also led to the English supporting Malcolm Canmore in his attempt to overthrow MacBeth.

It is impossible to put the story of MacBeth into perspective without remembering this basic fact of eleventh-century Scottish law: that the system was electoral and that the law of primogeniture was an alien concept. Dr Abraham Hume (*Who Was Macbeth?*, 1853) came close to understanding the different legal system when he wrote:

> The law of succession in the days of Kenneth MacAlpine was so peculiar that if we attempt to judge of it by modern instances, every step will be an error. Thus a brother of the last king was supposed to have a greater claim to the crown than a son; and for the same reason – i.e. that a youth might never sway the sceptre in preference to a man of mature years.

But Clayton Hutton (*Macbeth*, 1960) is typical of those who misunderstand the system and prefer to think that the simple, clear-cut law of primogeniture is a more advanced and civilized system:

> Nor was it true that the Crown that a new Scottish king put on his own head was normally passed down sedately from father to son. The unvarnished fact was that the thing was snatched and grabbed at like the oval ball in a Rugby football match at Murrayfield. ...
>
> No king of Scotland, in the days he [Shakespeare] was writing about, could expect to inherit the crown peacefully. Several families, branches descended from the Mac Alpins, took part in a villainous system in which they *elected* a king alternatively from one branch and then another.
>
> The king was supposed by ancient custom to be he who would be most likely, in modern language, to keep the gang in order.
>
> The system was another name for gangster rule. The king snatched the crown and throne by killing off his predecessor, and held them by defending his life against other attackers. He kept the crown and his life by killing off rivals before they could kill him.

Because the complicated electoral system of the Celts was not the familiar hereditary-feudal system practised elsewhere in Europe, Mr Hutton sweepingly concludes, 'There was no real legal succession in Scotland'. There is an element of truth in Mr Hutton's jaundiced view of the Celtic electoral system: a ruthless individual could abuse the system and, indeed, could 'snatch the crown and throne by killing off his predecessor'. That is precisely what Malcolm II did. But rulers who abused the system did not come along as often as Mr Hutton would have us believe, nor was their appearance due to the Celtic system or, as Mr Hutton would have it, lack of system. One only has to look at the royal succession in England, Norway and Denmark for a demonstration of the stability of the Celtic system.

As there was no such thing as primogeniture, there was also no such general conception as private property in land. The clan territory was not the property of the clan chieftain but was divided by the clan for the benefit of the community. Sections were appropriated by the chieftain and his 'civil service' in acknowledgement of their position in the society. Thereafter every clansman received a piece of land to work and develop. Another section was retained for the entire clan to use as common land. Yet another was set aside to support the poor and the old. All those clansmen who had their own plots were expected to pay taxes for the upkeep of the community, the support of the poor, the aged and orphans. But if a man fell behind with his taxes and died owing money, the surviving relatives were not made to pay his debts. Celtic law humanely stated that 'every dead man kills his liabilities'.

In this highly sophisticated and complex system of ownership there was no such thing as absolute ownership of land; the idea of private property was totally alien to the original Celtic system, although, about this time, such a concept was beginning to take root through the influence of the Christian Church. But no person could dispose of land without the common consent of the clan and even the disposal of chattels, such as cattle, was governed by various restrictions.

The principles of Celtic common ownership survived for a surprisingly long time in Scotland. William Skene, in *Celtic Scotland* (1876–80), states: 'Yet though the conscious Socialist movement be a century old, the labouring folk all down the ages have clung to communist practices and customs, partly the inheritance and instinct from the group and clan life of their forefathers and partly because these customs were their only barrier to poverty and because without them social life was impossible.' As late as 1847, says Skene, there were places in the Hebrides where the land was tilled, sowed and reaped in common and the produce divided among the workers equally, as it had been in MacBeth's time. The feast of *Nàbach* – from *Nàbaicheachd*, neighbourliness – was still held, when men drew their pieces of land by lot. The produce of certain lots was set aside for the poor and fines went to a common fund to buy fresh stock. John Rae, writing in the *Fortnightly Review* in 1895, says the communal system was then current in Islay and in St Kilda where they 'distributed the fishing rocks among themselves by lot', while in Barra 'they cast lots once a year for the several fishing grounds in the deep seas off their shores'.

The very basis of Celtic law was arbitration. The death penalty was enacted only in extreme cases and only when the guilty party was male. It was usual for the injured party to compel the wrong-doer to accept the arbitration and, under law, there was a custom of ritual fasting as a method of asserting one's rights.

As in all Celtic societies, women held an important place. A woman could be elected as a chieftain and even lead her clan into battle. She remained the owner of all she brought into a marriage; she could take office as the co-equal of man, and the electoral-inheritance system of chieftainship often passed through the female line as exemplified in the ancient sagas of the Ulster Cycle in Irish mythology. Women were well protected by law. Their status is given much attention in the seventh-century codification of the *Cáin Admomnáin*, which enumerates various fines against those who offend the honour of a woman. The *Cáin Admomnáin* specifically forbids the execution of a woman even if she is found guilty of premeditated murder. The most severe punishment prescribed by the law was banishment.

Under Celtic law 'medical service' was evolved in which sickness maintenance, including treatment, hospitalization and nourishing food were made available to all who needed it, irrespective of wealth and rank. This prototype 'National Health Service' was undoubtedly due in large part to the clan system, whereby a person was not just one of a large citizenry but a member of a particular clan, within which the clan made provision for the welfare of all its members. Both the ancient law tracts, the *Senchus Mór* and *Book of Aicill*, are explicit on the rights of the sick.

There were also strict laws concerning doctors, and anyone found practising medicine illegally or without the proper qualifications was liable to prosecution under the law.

It was into this country and this social system that MacBeth was born.

CHAPTER TWO

'Findlaech came from Scotland with an overwhelming army'
The Orkneyinga Saga

When Findlaech Mac Ruaridh and his wife Doada named their son MacBeth they chose a not uncommon name of the period. In Gaelic it is spelt Mac Bheatha (pronounced Mac Vah-ha) and it means 'the son of life'. It has been suggested that any name prefixed by the word *Mac* has to be a patronymic and, as MacBeth's father was Findlaech, some have suggested that the chroniclers have misspelt the name from Mael or Maol Bheatha, which would mean 'follower of life'. But we find the use of MacBeth occurring as a first name many times during this period. We also find the name disguised in a variety of anglicized spellings. There is a Magbiod who fought the Orkneymen in 980 and a Makepath listed as a distinguished prisoner after the battle of Neville's Cross in 1346. A MacBeth was Abbot of Iona and was slain there in 1070, while, during the reign of David I (1124–53), a MacBeth is on record as being one of the largest landowners in Edinburgh. Through anglicized phonetics the name Mac Bheatha has come down to English speakers not only as MacBeth but as McBey, MacVey and McVeagh.

Judging by a physical description, MacBeth Mac Findlaech was a handsome young man. St Berchan calls him a 'handsome youth', while other contemporary chroniclers such as Duan Albanach, Tighernach and Marianus Scotus, describe him as 'the red (haired) king', 'the liberal king ... fair, yellow and tall' and 'ruddy countenance, yellow hair and tall'.

13

Of MacBeth's mother, Doada, little is known except that she was the second daughter of Malcolm II. But of MacBeth's father we know much more. We know that Findlaech Mac Ruaridh was Mormaer of Moray and therefore one of the most powerful men in the kingdom next to the High King. We know that, apart from his connection by marriage to Malcolm II, Findlaech and the Mormaers of Moray before him had claims to the High Kingship and that contemporary chroniclers were so convinced of the justice of this claim that they frequently referred to the Mormaers of Moray as 'Kings of Alba'. We also know that the province of Moray, bordering on the territories of the jarls of the Orkneys, was often under attack by the Norsemen. An ancestor of MacBeth, also named MacBeth, is recorded as fighting against the Orkney Jarl, Skuli, in 976. Ten years before MacBeth was born, in 995, his own father, Findlaech, had to wage war against Jarl Sigurd Hlodversson. The outcome was decided at a battle fought at Skidmore in Caithness. According to the *Orkneyinga Saga*:

> It happened one summer that the earl who was called Findlaech came from Scotland with an overwhelming army. Findlaech challenged Sigurd to fight at Skidmore in Caithness and appointed a day for the battle.
> Jarl Sigurd collected an army. The Orkneymen were not eager to fight with superior numbers because it is said that the odds were not less than seven Scots to one of Sigurd's men. So the Jarl got no force from the Orkneys until he gave back to the farmers all their odal land in the islands to (induce them to serve in) his army. Then Sigurd went to battle with Findlaech and Sigurd had the victory, but the farmers got possession of the odal lands in the Orkneys.

The *Orkneyinga Saga* also relates that it was before this battle that Jarl Sigurd's mother made a new banner for her warrior son. 'The banner was made with great skill, and with excellent handiwork. It was made in the form of a raven; and when the wind blew out the banner it was as if the raven spread its wings.' The Saga says that no less than three of Sigurd's warriors were killed by Findlaech's men while bearing this standard forward. Sigurd himself fell while carrying this banner in the great battle with the Irish at Clontarf in 1014.

In the year that MacBeth was born his maternal grandfather,

Maol Cullum MacCoinneach, now remembered as Malcolm II, became High King of Scotland. Chroniclers are agreed that he was fifty-one years old when he ascended the throne at Scone. He was an ambitious man and not above abusing the weaknesses of the social system to obtain power, nor to retain it by judiciously removing his rivals. He became High King after defeating and killing Coinneach, or Kenneth III (997–1005), and his eldest son, Girc, in a battle at Monzievaird in Strathearn. The reason for the battle is not clear.

Although, by contemporary standards, an elderly man to succeed as High King, Malcolm showed himself to be an ambitious ruler. No sooner was he established at Scone than he led an army into Northumbria and besieged Durham. It was an unsuccessful attack and Earl Uchtred of Northumbria drove the Scots back. Nevertheless, so well did Malcolm conduct his campaign that the chroniclers were soon praising him as 'the most victorious king' and 'a warrior fortunate, praised of lords'.

Malcolm's first real test as a military commander came in 1009. Britain and Ireland were being subjected to savage assaults by the Danes and in that year Sweyn Forkbeard, King of Denmark, landed with an army on the coast of Moray Firth and laid siege to the township of Nairn. This, of course, was Findlaech's territory, but it would seem that the Moray clansmen were unable to cope with the Danish invaders by themselves and the Mormaer called upon his father-in-law, the High King, for help. Malcolm II marched an army to the Moray coast and managed to raise the siege of Nairn. The Danes reluctantly withdrew after bitter fighting. Malcolm was wounded in the conflict.

In the summer of the following year Sweyn Forkbeard made another assault on Moray, this time near Banff on the north coast. Malcolm gathered his clansmen and fought a battle at Mortlack. After a desperate struggle the Scots gained the upper hand and the Danes were once more driven back into the sea. In thanks for the victory, a grant of land was made to the great monastery of Deer, near Aberdeen. In later years a monument was erected at Mortlack to commemorate the victory. With these victories, Malcolm consolidated his domestic power and influence.

He had three children – all daughters – who were married into the three most powerful factions in Scotland.

Malcolm's eldest daughter, Bethoc, named after a popular Celtic saint, married Crinan, the Abbot of Dunkeld. Crinan appears in Irish texts by the more common name of Cronan but this misspelling occurred merely because Irish scribes were unfamiliar with the Scottish variant. As Abbot of Dunkeld, Crinan was one of the most powerful churchmen in Scotland. It must be remembered that at this time there was no rule against churchmen marrying in the Celtic Church. Some Gaelic names bear witness to this fact: names such as MacTaggart – Mac an tSagairt, 'son of the priest'. However, names such as MacPherson – Mac a' Phearsain, 'son of the parson', and MacPrior date from a later period. Even in the Roman Catholic Church in the early eleventh century married clergy could be found and, in 1050, Pope Leo IX was discussing ways and means of discouraging his priests from marrying. So Bethoc's marriage to the Abbot of Dunkeld was in no way unusual.

When John of Fordun (d. 1384) began to write his *Scotichronicon*, custom had changed drastically and he could not accept the concept of married clergy. He therefore deliberately 'corrected' Crinan's name and title to fall in with contemporary church custom. It was on Fordun that later historians began to base their erroneous image of MacBeth. Fordun's contemporary, Andrew of Wyntoun, was more liberal-minded and he made no bones about Bethoc's marriage to the Abbot.

The most important thing about Bethoc's marriage to Crinan was that he was also Mormaer of Atholl, the chief rival of Moray, and claimed a descent from the kings of Dalrada and the right to dominate the office of the High King. Crinan also claimed the title of 'Mormaer of the Isles'. While it is true that Atholl included Arran, Jura, Islay, Mull and Iona, the rest of the western isles were firmly under the rule of the jarls of the Orkneys, so the title seems to be wishful thinking on Crinan's part.

Crinan was also a warrior and had often led the Atholl clans into battle. He was thought to be descended from a man called Donnchadh ('brown warrior') who had also been Abbot of Dunkeld, and who was slain leading his clansmen into battle in 965. As a warrior Crinan seems to have acquired quite a reputation and the Norsemen came to know him as the Hound Earl – *Jarl Hundi*. The *Orkneyinga Saga* records how Crinan led a Scottish army northward to do battle with Sigurd Hlodversson, the Orkney Jarl, in 990. After an initial success the Scots were defeated at Dungal's Peak.

The marriage between Bethoc and Crinan, which took place around the year 1000, seems to have insured the wholehearted support of the Atholl clans for Malcolm II. The year after their marriage a son was born. He was called Donnchadh, after Crinan's ancestor, and is known by the anglicized version of his name – Duncan. Another son, Maldred, was born soon afterwards and then a daughter, whose name has not been recorded but who eventually married and was mother of a son named Moddan who was to play an important part in the events which led to MacBeth's succession.

Malcolm II's second daughter, Doada, married the powerful Mormaer of Moray, Findlaech Mac Ruaridh. MacBeth appears to have been their only child.

A third daughter, whose name is not recorded, was married into the third most powerful political faction affecting Scotland. Her husband was Sigurd Hlodversson, Jarl of the Orkneys, grandson of Thorfinn Skull-Crusher, the most feared of all Viking warriors. Sigurd was raised as a pagan, worshipping the ancient Norse gods. In about 995 he ransomed his life from the Christian King of Norway, Olaf Trygveson, by accepting Christianity as his faith and the faith of the people of Orkney. A Christian church was built at Birsay at his command. As a result of his change of religion Sigurd divorced his wife, Nereide, the sister of Jarl Gilli, who ruled the Hebrides from Colonsay on Sigurd's behalf. By his marriage to Nereide, Sigurd Hlodversson had three sons – Einar Wry-Mouth, Brusi and Sumarlidi. The *Orkneyinga Saga* records that Sigurd now 'married the daughter of Malcolm, King of the Scots, and their son was Jarl Thorfinn'. Thorfinn Sigurdsson was born before the winter of 1008 and his life was greatly to affect the future of the High Kings of Scotland.

In 1012, when MacBeth was seven years old, he was sent away to be educated, as prescribed by law. The term for this education was 'fosterage' and, as the son of an important chieftain, he would have been sent to one of the best teachers in the country, to live and study for about ten years. In the old pre-Christian society this teacher would have been a druid, but in eleventh-century

Scotland the teacher was usually a Christian monk – a culdee. This Celtic monastic order was founded in Dublin in 787 by St Maelruain and took its name from *Cele Dé*, Servant of God.

On his seventeenth birthday MacBeth reached *aimser togu*, the age of choice, and his education was formally finished. For a girl the *aimser togu* was reached at the age of fourteen. During his ten years of schooling MacBeth would have been educated in many subjects. He would have had to learn about the complicated legal system, for, if elected chieftain, it would be one of his duties to sit as a judge. He would have studied music and learnt to play an instrument – probably a form of harp – because music, both singing and playing an instrument, was considered an important accomplishment in Celtic society. Literature was another important field of study, especially poetry. There was a wealth of literature in Gaelic by this time. Scottish Gaelic shared with Manx and Irish a vast mythology. Irish has the oldest literary tradition in Europe, after Greek and Latin, and by MacBeth's day a great many of the sagas and legends had been committed to manuscript by monks who, while they tended to bowdlerize the ancient myths and cover them with a Christian veneer, preserved most of their vigour. The Gaelic of Scotland bore only a dialectical difference from Irish at this time and the written language could be fairly readily understood by either nationality. At this time Scotland was developing its own distinct written form of the language; but, alas, most of these manuscripts perished in the genocidal fanaticism of the Scottish Reformation during the sixteenth century. The ninth-century *Book of Deer* is the first surviving record of a language recognized as distinctly Scottish, as opposed to Irish or Manx.

Most importantly, MacBeth and his fellow students would have been instructed in the art of warfare, perhaps by warriors whose services were hired by the monks. MacBeth would have been taught the virtue of single combat by which an entire battle could be decided according to ancient Celtic tradition. There was no standing army in Scotland but each clansman had to be ready to serve in defence of his clan or national territory, which, in those days, was often threatened by the Vikings from the north and the Angles from the south.

Above all, the high value of honour would be impressed upon

him. One of the worst things that could befall a man in Celtic society was to be dishonoured, and a clansman was always ready to spring to arms to avenge any slight against himself or the things he held dear. As to weapons, MacBeth would have been taught proficiency with the sword. Most Celtic swords were long, and, according to Irish records, were often described as having hilts of gold, and were carried in sheaths of decorated bronze. Broad-bladed spears were often carried in battle, also a broad-bladed dagger. Rough wooden shields, mostly of alder wood with metal rims and elaborately decorated, were often used by chieftains, while small round targets of leather were carried by the clansmen. Scottish warriors preferred to wage war with swords and small shields. Neither bow, arrow nor body armour were to the clansmen's liking.

MacBeth would also have been taught recreational pursuits such as chess, as well as other board games which were peculiar to the Celts – games such as *fidchell*, 'wooden wisdom', and *brandub*, 'black raven'. Team games were also popular and a game similar to hurley (still played in Scotland and called *camanachd*) was the team game known as *báire*.

More to the young pupil's liking, perhaps, were the pleasures of hunting. He would have been taught how to snare wild birds, how to hunt boar and other game. But the favourite prey for the huntsman in Scotland was the wild deer. In Celtic mythology there occur many vivid descriptions of deer hunts. Apart from these pursuits, horse racing was always a major event in the ancient Celtic world.

Finally, the young MacBeth would have been given instruction in religion. Christianity had begun to spread in Scotland in 563 when an Irish monk named Colm, better known by his anglicized name of Columba, crossed to Scotland from Derry with some followers and established a Christian community on the tiny island of Iona, named I-Shona, the isle of saints. The Celtic Church that Columba established throughout all Scotland endured as the State Church in Scotland until Malcolm Canmore allowed his Saxon Queen Margaret to initiate its reformation in the latter part of the eleventh century. Even so, groups of culdees managed to survive until the fourteenth century.

The Celtic Church was monastic in form but its monasteries

were not for recluses. Rather they were religious settlements where men were educated to go out into the world and preach the Gospels. Under Celtic law the church lands were granted by the local clan from common stock, and the grants were made initially on the understanding that the land was not the private property of the church. The reforms of Queen Margaret altered all that.

As well as their native Gaelic, the monks were proficient in Latin, Hebrew and Greek, and it is likely that MacBeth also learnt these languages. Within the monastic communities all religious services were in Latin but, outside the monasteries, the monks carried out their proselytizing and worship in Gaelic.

The Celtic Church of MacBeth's day differed greatly from the Roman Church in practice and especially in the monks' tonsure, the theoretical celibacy of the Roman clergy and the date of the observance of Easter. In 463 Rome had adopted a new method of calculating Easter Day but the Celtic Church in Scotland, Ireland, Wales, Cornwall and Brittany retained the old computation. England, too, came under the supremacy of the Celtic Church in this matter until 664 when, at the Synod of Whitby, the English bishops declared in favour of the custom of the Church of Rome.

The primacy of the Celtic Church in Scotland was first established on Iona where all the lawful kings of Scotland were buried after St Colm's time. But in the early ninth century, because of increasing Danish raids on the island, the primacy was moved to Dunkeld, then to Abernethy and finally, in 908, to St Andrews.

By the eleventh century the Celtic Church had lost its hold in Wales and was losing it in Cornwall. In Brittany the bishops were fighting a losing battle to retain the old Celtic customs. In Ireland the church remained strong, and it was not until the middle of the century that the Irish church was finally led into the Roman fold by Maelmaedoc Ó Morgair (St Malachy). In Scotland at the beginning of the eleventh century the romanization of the Celtic Church was only a generation away.

Even though the Scottish Celtic Church was doggedly maintaining its independence at this time, it was, nevertheless, preparing the way for a revolution in Celtic law, land tenure and custom which would result in a feudal society being established in Scotland after the fall of MacBeth. Whereas previously each clan had its own priests and bishops, the diocese being the district occupied by the clan, and each clan allotted lands for the support of its clergy, the Church now began to advocate the introduction of private property and land feudalization. The concepts of private property and primogeniture were brought from Europe by returning missionaries; the titles of landholders, once temporary, were hardening into permanent ownership, and in parts of the country, particularly in the south, the old communal clan ownership became in many cases little more than a superior jurisdiction, the exercise of which was rarely invoked.

CHAPTER THREE

'Sword blades rang on Ireland's coast'

Njal's Saga

On 23 April, 1014, an event took place in Ireland which was to have great significance for Scotland. At the Battle of Clontarf the Celts, led by the High King of Ireland, Brían Boroimhe (Brian Boru), smashed for ever Norse hopes of dominating Ireland. The Norsemen had established various semi-independent settlements in Ireland at Dublin, Wexford, Waterford, Cork and Limerick. When Brían became High King in 1002 he exerted his power over all the Irish kingdoms and over 'the kingdoms of the foreigners', the Norse settlements.

However, Brían's wife, Gormflaith, was a sister of Maelmore, the provincial king of Leinster. She had, in turn, been the wife of Olaf, the Norse king of Dublin, of Mael Sechnaill, a former High King, and lastly of Brían himself. A quarrel seems to have taken place between Gormflaith and Brían as a result of which she conspired to overthrow him. She incited her brother, Maelmore, to rebel and enticed her son by Olaf, Sigtrygg, or Sitric, Silken-Beard, who was now king of Dublin, to join the rebellion. The two kings were too weak to act against Brían on their own, so they sent word to the Vikings to come to Ireland and overthrow the High King. The Norsemen gathered from far and wide – from the Isle of Man, the Hebrides, from Norway, from Denmark and even from the Baltic. But, most important, in Scotland's case, they came from the Orkneys.

Sigurd Hlodversson, Jarl of the Orkneys, accepted an offer from Sigtrygg to become the supreme commander of the Norse forces. Before he left for Ireland, Sigurd sent his wife and young son, Thorfinn, to his father-in-law, Malcolm II, at Scone.

Brían, who was about seventy-two years old, appealed to the Celtic world for allies to help him repel the Norse invasion. Malcolm II, in spite of his relationship to Jarl Sigurd, responded immediately. A large Scottish contingent, commanded by Domhnall Mac Eimin Mac Cainnich, the Mormaer of Cé (Marr and Buchan), was sent to Ireland to join Brían's forces. It is likely that Malcolm was farsighted enough to see that, if the Norsemen controlled Ireland, Scotland would soon be isolated and surrounded by Norse-controlled countries and, under such circumstances, it would not retain its independence for long.

The battle began at dawn on Good Friday, 23 April, 1014, at Clontarf, just outside Dublin. By evening the routed Norsemen were escaping to their longboats. The rebel Irish king, Maelmore, was dead and the supreme commander of the Norsemen, Sigurd Hlodversson, was lying on the field of battle where he had been slain leading a charge with his famous 'raven banner' in his hands.

On Brían's side there was also a terrible slaughter. Brían's son, Murchadh, the commander of the Irish forces, was killed, as was Turloch, Brían's sixteen-year-old grandson. The Mormaer of Cé, commanding the Scottish forces, was also killed. But the biggest blow for the Irish was the death of Brían himself, slain by a Manx chieftain named Brodir while he was standing at the door of his tent awaiting news of the battle in which he had been unable to take part because of his great age.

Nevertheless, the power of the Norsemen in Ireland was smashed forever. The High Kingship of Ireland went to Mael Sechnaill who ruled until 1022. The Norsemen left Ireland and Scotland alone and turned to easier conquests. *Njal's Saga* records of Clontarf:

> Sword blades rang on Ireland's coast.
> Metal yelled as shield it sought,
> Spear-points in the well-armed host.
> I heard sword-blows many more;
> Sigurd fell in battle's blast,
> From his wounds there sprang hot gore.
> Brían fell, but won at last.

The *Orkneyinga Saga* tells us that Thorfinn Sigurdsson, at his grandfather's court at Scone, was only 'five winters' old when the news of Clontarf reached Scotland. Malcolm II, now preoccupied with plans to expand and unite the territories of Scotland into one great kingdom, realized that the Orkneys, with their territories on the Scottish mainland and the western isles, would be an excellent addition to his kingdom. But his young grandson Thorfinn was the fourth and youngest of Sigurd Hlodversson's sons and already the three sons by Sigurd's first wife, Nereide, were dividing up the Orkney jarldom between them. The *Orkneyinga Saga* says of these brothers:

> Einar was a hard, ambitious man, cantankerous and a great fighter. Brusi was a mild man, equable of temper, unfettered and of good conversation. Sumarlidi was more like Brusi in character. He was the eldest of the brothers and the shortest lived. He died in bed.

The fact that his grandson was the youngest of the dead jarl's sons, and that the law of primogeniture was observed by the Norsemen, did not deter Malcolm. The *Orkneyinga Saga* says that he 'bestowed Caithness and Sutherland upon him (Thorfinn) with the title of earl and gave him men to rule the domain along with him'. Obviously Malcolm took advantage of the shock of Sigurd's death to exert a claim to suzerainty over Caithness and Sutherland and then bestow this claim on Thorfinn. However, the claim to suzerainty was dubious, because, under Celtic law, Malcolm had no right to bestow any lands or titles in this manner. Perhaps the bestowal was allowed because Caithness and Sutherland, as part of the Orkney jarldom, were not governed by Celtic law. Nor could Malcolm make Thorfinn an 'earl' as no such title existed within the Celtic system. Whatever the illegalities of the situation, it is true that Malcolm established his young grandson as ruler of the Caithness and Sutherland territory while Thorfinn's three half-brothers were squabbling about the division in the islands.

Malcolm displayed much wisdom in seeing the drawbacks in bringing up Thorfinn at Scone in a Gaelic environment, away from Norse culture. If Thorfinn was to become ruler of the jarldom of the Orkneys, he would have to be acceptable to the Norse inhabitants and that meant that he had to be raised as a

Norseman and not as a Scot. Malcolm therefore sent his grandson, presumably with his mother, to live in Caithness with sufficient warriors to protect the boy from any aggression by his half-brothers. In Caithness Thorfinn grew to manhood as a Norse jarl. We are told that 'Jarl Thorfinn developed early and was the tallest and strongest of men, with black hair (sharp features and grisly aspect). And when he grew up it was obvious that he was of ambitious and warlike disposition'. Malcolm was content to wait until the boy was old enough to challenge his half-brothers for the entire jarldom and, if he were successful, Malcolm hoped his grandson would acknowledge his debt to him and recognize his ultimate authority as High King.

While Malcolm was scheming to expand his borders in the north, events were taking place in England which were to lead to an expansion of his southern borders. Sweyn Forkbeard, King of the Danes, having suffered two successive defeats in Scotland, had turned his ambitious eyes on England. In the middle of July, 1013, Sweyn and his son, Canute, led a Danish invasion against the English King, Ethelred, on the pretext that Ethelred had massacred Danish settlers in England; his invasion was to exact revenge. By the autumn of that year Sweyn was master of all England with the exception of London, where Ethelred was putting up a stubborn resistance. The situation was hopeless and Ethelred's queen, Emma of Normandy, and her two sons, Edward and Alfred, had already fled the country. In January, 1014, Ethelred followed her into exile in Normandy.

Sweyn Forkbeard now declared himself King of England as well as Denmark. His success was short-lived for he died on 3 February, 1014, at Gainsborough. His son, Canute, then declared himself king, but Ethelred, seizing on the uncertainty of the situation, returned to England to lead an uprising against him. Ethelred died on 23 April, 1016, and the English parliament, the Witenagemot, proclaimed his eldest son, Edmund, his successor. But on 30 November, 1016, Edmund died and English resistance to Canute died with him. Canute now divided the country into four great earldoms. Wessex he kept for himself; East Anglia he gave to Thorkell; Mercia to Eadric and Northumbria to Eric – all loyal Danish warriors. Canute further ensured his position by marrying Ethelred's widow, Emma of Normandy, in July, 1017.

Emma was by no means inconsolable at the death of Ethelred. In fact she had always despised him and her marriage to Canute seemed to ensure that the claims of Ethelred's sons to the English throne were not seriously considered.

The warfare which ravaged England suited Malcolm II's territorial ambitions. He took advantage of the fact that Canute had slain his old adversary, Earl Uchtred of Northumbria, and given the earldom to a Dane. While Northumbria was torn by strife between Eric and the English half-brother of Uchtred, Eadulf Cudel, who was still holding the Northumbrian territory north of the River Tyne, Malcolm marched an army southwards. His eyes were on the former kingdom of Bernica, which had been a Brythonic Celtic region until settled by Angles and Flemings as early as 547. Celts and Angles had struggled for domination of the territory until, early in the seventh century, the Angles won a decisive victory over the Celts at Dawstone. They then set themselves up as the ruling class in the area; but the majority of peasants and labourers were still Celtic.

Malcolm realized the strategic importance of the territory and this was, perhaps, his main reason for its annexation. He must also have judged that the majority of the people in the territory, being Celtic, resented life under an alien feudal system and would welcome a Scottish take-over.

Malcolm's army marched to Carham, a few miles above Coldstream, where they encountered the Northumbrian army of Eadulf Cudel in 1018. Symeon of Durham says:

> A comet appeared for thirty nights to the people of Northumbria, a terrible presage of the calamity by which that province was about to be desolated. For shortly afterwards (that is, after thirty days) nearly the whole population, from the River Tees to the Tweed and the borders, were cut off in which they were engaged with a countless multitude of Scots at Carham.

The Northumbrians were defeated and Eadulf Cudel was forced to surrender Bernica. It has remained an integral part of Scotland ever since. Although Symeon of Durham fiercely rebukes Eadulf Cudel for his cowardice in surrendering the territory, he fails to make clear how, after a military defeat by the Scots, and with Eric and a Danish army pressing upward from the south, he could have held on to the land.

With the victory of the Scots at Carham, the territory ruled by the High Kings of Scotland achieved its greatest expansion to the south. Professor Kenneth Jackson, in *The Celtic Aftermath in the Islands*, affirms that 'in consequence of this [Carham] the whole of Scotland became for a time Gaelic in speech'. This fact, which we will deal with in more detail later, can be readily confirmed by the extent of Gaelic place-names in the area that originate from this period.

CHAPTER FOUR

'The Man of the Sword,
Seeking Scotland's throne,
Ever won victory...'

Arnor the Skald

In 1020, when MacBeth was fifteen years old, his father, Finlaech Mac Ruaridh, was killed by his nephews, Malcolm and Gillecomgain, the sons of his brother, Maelbrighde. The only conclusion one can draw as to why they would want to kill their uncle is that he had become too friendly with the House of Atholl. He had married Malcolm II's daughter, Doada, and had twice relied on the aid of the High King during the Danish raids of 1009 and 1010, placing himself and his clans under Malcolm's command. It must be remembered that the House of Moray maintained a fierce independence and claimed an equal if not higher right to the High Kingship than the House of Atholl. It could have been that Findlaech's nephews resented the Mormaer's connections with Scone. Or had he transgressed his office in some other way?

Certainly the contemporary chroniclers did not record any opposition when Malcolm Mac Maelbrighde had himself elected Mormaer of Moray. Malcolm ruled the province for nine years before he died, seemingly of natural causes, in 1029. His brother, Gillecomgain, was then elected to the office.

Gillecomgain appears to have been a very determined and independent ruler, incurring Malcolm II's displeasure by pursuing Moray's claim to the High Kingship. He strengthened this claim by marrying Gruoch, the granddaughter of Kenneth III, whom Malcolm II had slain in 1005. Gruoch and her brother,

Malcolm Mac Bodhe, were the only children of Bodhe, one of the four sons of Kenneth III. Malcolm II, in his climb to power, made sure that Kenneth and his four sons were eliminated. However, he seems to have overlooked the survival of Kenneth's grandchildren. While, as we know, there was no hereditary system, obviously Gruoch and her brother were symbols of resistance to Malcolm II. Gillecomgain certainly improved his position by his union with Gruoch who bore him a son, Lulach, in 1031.

What happened to MacBeth after his father was killed? For a while he vanishes from the pages of the chronicles. He was probably away at the time, still pursuing his 'fosterage'. Possibly his education could have been at Scone itself, at the court of Malcolm II, for he was certainly at Scone in 1031. However, we must not anticipate.

While the fortunes of MacBeth apparently declined, those of his cousin Thorfinn Sigurdsson improved. The rise of Thorfinn to power in the Orkneys was of prime importance to MacBeth's eventual succession to the throne, so to dwell on Thorfinn's rise is not to digress from the main story. Fortunately, a detailed account of Thorfinn Sigurdsson's life is given in the *Orkneyinga Saga*, which deals with the history of the jarldom of the Orkneys over a period of three centuries from the tenth century onward, though scholars accept that it was probably not written down until the twelfth century. Certainly it was quoted by a chronicler in the middle of the thirteenth century, although the oldest surviving manuscript belongs to the fourteenth century. It seems to have first been committed to writing in Iceland, for the earliest manuscripts are Icelandic and, with the notable exceptions of Turf Einar and Rognvald Kali, the majority of skalds or poets whose works are quoted as part of the sagas are Icelandic. Poets were the original authors, the manuscripts being composed of the sagas of individual poets which were then collected and transcribed by one man. Alexander Burt Taylor, in *The Orkneyinga Saga: A New Translation with Introduction and Notes*, (Edinburgh, 1938) claims that this single transcriber of the oral poetic tradition was not a churchman but a layman, 'a man of considerable wealth and importance. He possessed, or had access, to a collection of Kings' Sagas. He was able to travel widely, and meet the most notable families in Caithness and the Orkneys. He is quite at home in tales of earls and kings and large landowners'. Whoever this man was, we are grateful to him for his detailed narrative of the rise of MacBeth's cousin, Thorfinn. Living with his mother in the Norse province of Caithness and Sutherland, young Thorfinn had been lucky in finding a substitute for his father, a man who undertook his education not just in things academic but in the military arts and in politics. This man was Thorkell Amundisson, whose father was rich and influential in Sandwick. Thorkell, according to the *Orkneyinga Saga*, was 'in every way the most accomplished of men born and bred in the Orkneys'. But Thorkell had run into trouble with Thorfinn's half-brother, Einar Wry-Mouth, who, of the three sons of Nereide and Sigurd, had come to dominate the Orkney jarldom. Thorkell clashed with Einar over what he considered to be unjust taxes levied on the people. He pleaded at a *thing* (a Norse parliament) that Einar should revoke certain of these taxes. In this he incurred Einar's intense hatred and was advised to leave the Orkneys for a time.

Thorkell therefore went to Caithness and joined the household of the young Thorfinn Sigurdsson. He undertook Thorfinn's education and thereafter became known to the saga writers as Thorkell Fosterer, 'and he was the most estimable of men'.

About the time that Thorfinn was fourteen years old his half-brother Sumarlidi died. Thorfinn immediately sent a message to his surviving half-brothers, Einar and Brusi, claiming Sumarlidi's third share of the jarldom. Einar replied that Thorfinn already called himself Jarl of Caithness and Sutherland and had the protection of his grandfather, the High King of Scotland. Caithness and Sutherland had been ruled by Sigurd and was already larger than a third part of the islands. Therefore, said Einar, Thorfinn already had his share of the jarldom and he would receive no more. The saga writer, showing his bias, adds that Einar 'was very unfair in his distribution of plunder'. Brusi, however, said he was quite willing to give up any territory providing it was not his third share of the inheritance. 'It is not my will,' he said, 'to covet more of the realm than the third which I hold by right.' But the decision seems to have lain in the hands of Einar Wry-Mouth.

Having received this rebuff, Thorfinn, with the aid and advice of Thorkell Fosterer, collected a small army from Caithness and Sutherland. It is also recorded that Malcolm II expressed his willingness to raise the Scottish clans to help his grandson against Einar. Obviously his motive in this was to break the power of the Orkney jarldom and, by placing Thorfinn in control, bring the jarldom under the control of Scone.

Thorfinn's expedition sailed for the Orkneys. The saga writers confirm that Thorfinn Sigurdsson was only fourteen years old when he led the expedition which would have made the year 1022, although the same writers record the year as 1020. However, the actual dates given in the sagas are variable.

According to Arnor the Skald, who became Thorfinn's personal poet:

> Reddened the sword's edge,
> Did the Prince in the helmet storm.
> Reddener of raven's claws
> Yet of fifteen winters,
> No man under the Heaven
> Younger than Einar's brother
> Ready has shown himself –
> Valiant and stout of heart –
> To defend and conquer.

Einar gathered an army to meet Thorfinn but Brusi intervened and acted as a mediator between the two of them. Thanks to Brusi's efforts, a settlement was reached between all three brothers whereby each of them had a third share of the jarldom but Einar Wry-Mouth was to be overlord of the islands and responsible for their defence. It was also agreed that, if one brother died, his lands would be divided between the surviving brothers.

Thorfinn returned to Caithness. The following year he sent Thorkell Fosterer to the Orkneys to claim his *skatt*, the income from his third share of the jarldom. Einar Wry-Mouth was antagonistic and charged Thorkell with being the initiator of Thorfinn's seizure of a share of the jarldom. Thorkell, his life threatened, fled from the Orkneys and returned to Caithness. Thorfinn told him to go to Norway to discuss the matter with

King Olaf II. Olaf had actually seized power in Norway while Canute, who claimed suzerainty over the country, was away subduing England. It chanced that Olaf had quarrelled with Einar Wry-Mouth and Thorfinn probably saw the animosity between them as a means of weakening his half-brother's position. The animosity had nearly resulted in open warfare during recent years after Einar Wry-Mouth had murdered a close friend of Olaf's named Evyand Urus-Horn.

The saga writers record that Thorkell Fosterer went to see Olaf in the autumn and stayed with the Norwegian King 'in high favour' through the winter. In the spring Olaf invited Thorfinn to come and stay with him. Some sort of agreement was evidently reached by which the Norwegian King promised Thorfinn his support and friendship in any moves he might make against Einar Wry-Mouth. The saga writers say of Thorfinn's visit that 'he was welcomed cordially, and stayed there well through the summer. And when he got ready to return to the west, King Olaf gave him a large and fine warship fully equipped.' Thorkell Fosterer also returned with Thorfinn.

Returning in the autumn, Thorfinn went straight to the Orkneys and demanded his entitlement from Einar Wry-Mouth. Einar reacted by assembling his warriors and once again Brusi had to intervene to prevent a conflict. 'And the upshot was that they came to terms and confirmed it between them with oaths,' says the saga writer. 'Thorkell Fosterer was to keep peace and friendship with Jarl Einar and it was laid down that each should entertain the other at a feast and that the Jarl should make the first visit to Thorkell at Sandwick.'

Thorkell had evidently inherited his father's house at Sandwick on South Ronaldsay. Whether Thorfinn was a party to subsequent events we shall never know but it is likely that what happened was the outcome of a secret plan between Thorfinn, Thorkell and Olaf. Thorkell Fosterer prepared a feast for Einar Wry-Mouth at Sandwick. The Jarl, unsuspecting, went unarmed into the feasting hall with his attendants. Thorkell then managed to separate Einar from his men and slew him in the presence of 'a man called Hallvard, an Icelander from the Eastern Fjords', obviously an accomplice. Einar's men stood by helplessly as Thorkell and his armed supporters pushed their way out of the house and down to where his longboat rode at anchor. According to the *Orkneyinga Saga*:

> Thorkell then went to his ship and the Jarl's men dispersed. That very day Thorkell set sail towards the east. It was towards the end of October. He landed safe and sound in Norway and went immediately to see King Olaf and had a cordial welcome. The King approved of the deed and Thorkell stayed with him that winter.

Meanwhile Brusi, probably realizing that his peace plans were all for nothing and that Thorfinn, as ambitious and ruthless as Einar, was behind the killing, now took Einar's inheritance and refused to share the jarldom with his half-brother. A *thing* was held to discuss the matter. Brusi argued:

> I am content to have the third of the land which I inherited from my father; and no one had challenged my right to this. But now I have inherited another third from my brother by lawful settlement. But though I am unable to try conclusion with thee, brother, yet I will seek another's help than yield up my realm on such terms.

Brusi's threat to 'seek another's help' was based on the mistaken notion that he could appeal to King Olaf of Norway for assistance. Thorfinn was now threatening war and had amassed a large army, probably about five to ten thousand men, ready to embark for the Orkneys. Among them was a contingent of clansmen supplied by Malcolm II. In the face of this threat, Brusi embarked for Norway, taking his ten year old son, Rognvald, with him. Thorfinn, secure in the knowledge of his secret agreement with Olaf of Norway, leisurely made his way to the Orkneys, landed unopposed and then followed Brusi to Olaf's court.

Unbeknown to Thorfinn, however, King Olaf had entered the power struggle for the Orkney jarldom on his own account. Instead of supporting Thorfinn, he told Brusi that the kings of Norway had a just claim over the Orkneys. As ruler of Norway, he, Olaf, was quite willing that Brusi remain jarl of the islands, provided that Brusi swore allegiance to Norway and shared the income of the islands with him:

> I will give thee the option, that thou become my man, when of course I shall give the isle to thee in fief. Then we shall see whether my assistance will stand thee in better stead than the support of the

King of Scots will thy brother Thorfinn. But if thou wilt not have this option, then I shall see about recovering the ownership and *odal* rights which up till now my kinsmen and forefathers have held in the west.

Brusi was puzzled by the alternatives offered by Olaf. He retired to consult his followers, telling them what Olaf had offered. He told them:

> But I am quite in the dark as to what will happen to me at our parting if I say 'no' to him, since the King had openly declared that claim which he has on the Orkneys. But what with his own ambition and the fact that we have come here, he would not scruple to deal as he liked with our decision.

After much consideration, Brusi agreed to become the liegeman of King Olaf. The Orkneys would henceforth be part of Norway. At this point Thorfinn arrived at the Norwegian court. Word had probably reached him that Olaf was pursuing his own ambitions, but when he arrived he must have been taken aback to learn that King Olaf had come to an agreement with Brusi. But Olaf was not done with intriguing. He now put similar proposals before Thorfinn. Norway would exercise control over the Orkneys and Brusi was to have one-third of the jarldom, Thorfinn one-third and the remaining third would go to Olaf.

Thorfinn was naturally angry at this double-dealing. He refused to accept the proposal and significantly pointed out that he could not accept Norwegian control over the Orkneys because he had already accepted Scotland's right to the islands. The saga writer puts these words into his mouth:

> And, sir, if thou expectest to need my support against other chiefs then thou hast fully secured it. But it is impossible for me to pay thee homage for I am already a jarl of the King of Scots and a vassal of his.

Olaf was an astute ruler and, rather than have an immediate confrontation, he gave Thorfinn time to think the matter over. During this time Thorkell Fosterer, then living at Olaf's court, advised Thorfinn to agree to Olaf's terms. Thorfinn finally did agree and the saga writer noted that 'the King observed that Thorfinn was made of sterner stuff than Brusi and had less liking for such coercion as this.' As soon as the official agreement had been made, Thorfinn and Thorkell sailed west. Brusi sailed later, leaving his young son Rognvald to be raised at the Norwegian court. The *Orkneyinga Saga* says:

> He (Rognvald) was the most handsome of men, with long golden hair like silk. He was tall and strong for his years, and the most accomplished of men both in understanding and manners. He lived a long time with King Olaf.

For a time Thorfinn Sigurdsson settled down in Caithness while Brusi returned to live in the Orkneys.

The settlement was surely not to the liking of Malcolm. However, there is no record of the elderly High King's reaction to his grandson's switch of allegiance from Scotland to Norway and the settlement did bring a period of peace.

In 1028 there was another significant shift in the balance of power which was to benefit Thorfinn Sigurdsson and lay another important paving stone on the road of MacBeth's rise to power. Canute of England and Denmark reasserted his old claim to the kingship of Norway. He invaded Olaf's kingdom with twenty-eight ships of war, having made lengthy preparations for the invasion, promising various Norse jarls money and position if they betrayed their king. One of the most important factors behind Canute's success was the reaction of the Norwegians to the imposition of Christianity on their country by King Olaf and his predecessors. Many Norwegians were still hostile to the new religion, and even the ordinary folk resented the imperious way Christianity had been thrust upon them.

Therefore, when Canute landed in Norway King Olaf found himself almost deserted. With a few faithful followers, he fled across the mountains to Sweden and finally took refuge in Kiev where his brother-in-law, Jaroslav, was king. Canute, on returning to England, left Haakon Eriksson as his regent in Norway. But Haakon did not enjoy power for long. He perished in a shipwreck and Canute then sent his young son, Sweyn, to act as regent. Sweyn was Canute's son by his first wife, Aelfgifu, who now accompanied her son to his new appointment. They had barely reached the Vik, in the southern part of the country, when they heard the news that Olaf was returning with a fresh army.

It was Haakon's death which encouraged Olaf's attempt to win back the throne now that Canute had returned to England. Olaf's army met Sweyn's forces on 29 July, 1030, at Stiklestad, where rich meadows slope gently towards the shore at the head of Trondheim Fjord. Olaf faced an army twice the size of his own. Tradition says that he fell at the spot where a tiny eleventh-century church now stands.

Sweyn established a rule far more arbitrary than Olaf had ever exercised, and at once people began to create legends about the king they had deposed. Such a folklore grew up around the dead Olaf that, on 3 August, 1041, Bishop Grimkell declared the dead Norwegian King to be a saint.

The importance of these events in Norway lay in the fact that the Orkneys were freed from Norwegian control and Olaf no longer took a third of the revenue. In fact the Orkneys were entirely forgotten, leaving Thorfinn free to pursue his policy of trying to oust his half-brother, Brusi.

While his son Sweyn was consolidating the new conquest, Canute went on a pilgrimage to Rome. According to the *Anglo-Saxon Chronicle*:

> King Canute went to Rome and as soon as he came home he went to Scotland, and the Scots King, Malcolm, submitted to him and became his man but held that only a little while; and two other kings, Maelbeatha and Jehmarc.

The date of Canute's visit to Scotland was 1031 but there is no evidence that he went at the head of an invading army or that any battles were fought of such significance as to force Malcolm II to acknowledge Canute as his overlord. And surely Malcolm, with his drive and ambition, would not have meekly submitted his kingdom to Canute without any attempt to protect it? Such an invasion would have been noticed by other contemporary chroniclers. The *Anglo-Saxon Chronicle* is more than likely boasting or has misinterpreted the reason behind Canute's journey to Scotland. Without the evidence of a military invasion, it seems likely that Canute went to see Malcolm on an equal footing, one ruler to another, to see whether Scotland had any designs on England, or even whether some alliance could be formed. Malcolm probably assured Canute that he had no more territorial ambitions towards the south and that he could count on friendly relations with Scotland. In this way would Malcolm have 'become his man'. After all, if Canute had gone north with an army, defeated Malcolm (in spite of the silence of contemporary chroniclers) and made the Scottish king submit to English domination, the first thing that Northumbria would have done would have been to reclaim the Bernican territory. Later historians, seeking an explanation for Canute's journey to Scotland, maintain that it was precisely for this reason that Canute went; that is to punish the Scots for the Northumbrian defeat at Carham. But that was certainly not done and the territory remained part of Scotland.

The importance of the passage in the *Anglo-Saxon Chronicle* lies in the mention of the two 'kings' who were introduced by Malcolm to Canute – Maelbeatha, obviously MacBeth, and Jehmarc. In other chronicles they are described as 'kings of the north'. Caradoc of Llancarvon was more specific and stated that Maelbeatha was 'king of the Orkneys' and that Jehmarc was 'king of Uist'. In no way could MacBeth have been 'king of the Orkneys' unless, as a reaction to Thorfinn's switch of allegiance to Norway, Malcolm designated his other grandson, MacBeth, as jarl of the Orkneys. This seems rather unlikely and out of keeping with Celtic law, although, as has been shown, Malcolm was not above twisting the law to his own ends.

Perhaps the simple explanation is that MacBeth, with Jehmarc, was staying at Scone as part of the High King's family and, for presentation purposes, was introduced to the King of England in vague terms as a northern chieftain. This description was then recorded and translated in terms of English nobility by the author of the *Anglo-Saxon Chronicle* and later echoed by the historian William of Malmesbury.

A significant event in MacBeth's life was recorded in the *Annals of Ulster* for the following year, 1032: 'Gillecomgain, Mormaer of Moray, son of Maelbrighde, was burned (to death) along with fifty of his warriors'. Gillecomgain, with fifty of his clansmen, had been surprised in his fortress by Atholl clansmen, perhaps under orders from Malcolm II himself, and killed. It was merely another incident in the conflict between Moray and Atholl. The previous major incident had taken place in 1027 when Dunkeld, with its monastery and churches, the seat of the

Mormaer of Atholl, was 'entirely burnt'. The struggle between Moray and Atholl was growing more acute. Malcolm was growing old, he was already in his late seventies, and naturally worried about the succession. According to the tanistry system, specifically the Celtic law of *geilfine*, whereby a ruler, whether he be a clan chieftain or king, nominates his successor before his death, Malcolm had already nominated his eldest grandson, Duncan, the son of Crinan, Mormaer of Atholl, as his successor. Obviously Malcolm could not know whether Duncan would be elected, for the nomination depended upon acceptance by the chieftains and churchmen. The nominee had to have his claim discussed by a gathering of mormaers, chieftains and churchmen at an assembly and a vote taken. And, if there were better qualified candidates, then Duncan might not succeed to the High Kingship at all.

In the eyes of the ambitious and ruthless Malcolm, the simple answer was to eliminate the opposition. And it was in Moray that the strongest opposition lay. The Mormaer, Gillecomgain, not only personified the Moray claim but he also had the support of those who had opposed Malcolm's deposal of Kenneth III, for Gillecomgain had married Kenneth's granddaughter, Gruoch. It is likely that Malcolm tried to eliminate Gillecomgain, Gruoch and their son, Lulach, in one lightning raid on Gillecomgain's fortress near Inverness. But, though the Mormaer and fifty of his warriors perished in the flames of the fort, Gruoch and her son managed to escape.

In the following year, 1033, Malcolm succeeded in murdering Malcolm Mac Bodhe, Gruoch's brother, who, it seems, had the strongest chance of defeating Duncan at the electoral assembly.

It is now that MacBeth begins to appear on the canvas of history. Following the death of his cousin, Gillecomgain, MacBeth was elected Mormaer of Moray. However, if, after the killing of his father, Findlaech, by Malcolm and Gillecomgain Mac Maelbrighde, MacBeth was brought up at Scone, under the influence of Malcolm II, is it not possible that he had been a party to the murder of Gillecomgain and Malcolm Mac Bodhe? At first glance it would seem a natural assumption, because the slaying of Gillecomgain by MacBeth would then be a simple act of revenge for Gillecomgain's part in the slaying of Findlaech Mac Ruaridh.

My personal conjecture is that MacBeth was not a party to the murder of Gillecomgain nor of Malcolm Mac Bodhe and that both were instigated by the House of Atholl to ensure Duncan's succession. This conjecture is based on the fact that when MacBeth was elected Mormaer of Moray, on the death of Gillecomgain, there is no record of dissension by the Moray clans. MacBeth continued to pursue hostile relationships with the House of Atholl and even married Gruoch and adopted her child, Lulach. If he had been Malcolm II's 'man' this *volte-face* would have been astonishing. As for Gruoch, who must in no way be confused with the Shakespearian image of 'Lady Macbeth', it seems unlikely that she would have married the murderer of her husband or her brother. She clearly represented the anti-Atholl faction and would certainly not have accepted MacBeth if he were merely the tool of Atholl politics.

So, by 1033, the twenty-eight-year-old MacBeth had become Mormaer of Moray and, according to contemporary chroniclers, 'King of Alba'. He had married Gruoch, granddaughter of Kenneth III, and adopted her son. He had a right to consider himself as candidate for the High Kingship, not only as chief of the House of Moray but as a descendant of Atholl as well, being the grandson of Malcolm II. He had the necessary family qualifications and, as it turned out, the capability to fulfil the office of the High King. But, before Malcolm came to regard his grandson as a threat to Duncan's succession, the old king was dead.

On 25 November, 1034, aged eighty, Malcolm II died at Glammis. Hundreds of years later some historians tried to claim that he was 'slain treacherously', but the tale is inconsistent with contemporary sources, all of which agree that he died naturally. He had been ambitious and greedy but his ruthlessness had aided him in holding on to the territory he had gained and he had been successful in defending his territory against foreign invasion. His successor was to share that ambition and greed but lacked the ruthlessness and strength of character.

Under the Celtic law of *geilfine* Duncan Mac Crinan had been nominated his successor. It is not recorded whether Moray contested the election, but certainly, just before Christmas, 1034, Duncan was acclaimed High King at Scone. He was thirty-three years old. He had been married four years earlier to a Danish woman, a cousin of Jarl Siward, a warrior at the court of Canute of England and a man who was soon to make himself Earl of Northumbria.

Before his election as High King, Duncan had been provincial king of Cumbria. This office now passed to his younger brother, Maldred Mac Crinan, who had forged strong ties with the old English ruling families of Northumbria. He had married Aldgytha, a daughter of Earl Uchtred, whose brother Eadulf had now replaced Eric the Dane as earl. Aldgytha was the granddaughter of Ethelred II of England. Maldred's family survived into the twelfth century as earls of Northumbria.

With Duncan finally acclaimed as High King, the House of Atholl was firmly in the ascendant. But events outside the country were soon to be felt by the new High King of Scotland.

In 1035 Canute of England died at Shaftesbury and was buried at Winchester. He was about forty years old. There was now a crisis as to who should succeed to the throne of England. Canute had two sons by his first wife, Aelfgifu – Sweyn and Harald Harefoot, and one son by his second wife, Emma of Normandy – Hardicanute. Hardicanute was in Denmark with Sweyn. The English Witenagemot declared in favour of Hardicanute but appointed Harald Harefoot as regent until he returned. Harald used this time to persuade the Witenagemot to appoint him king because of his half-brother's absence, due to a successful insurrection in Norway. The Norwegians, regretting the overthrow of Olaf, which had made way for the arbitrary rule of Canute's son, Sweyn, supported an insurrection which placed Olaf's young son, Magnus, on the throne. Led by Einar and Kalv Arnisson, the same jarls who had commanded the army which defeated Olaf, the insurrectionary group brought the eleven-year-old Magnus to Norway in the summer of 1035, while Sweyn, and his mother, Aelfgifu, fled to Denmark where Hardicanute joined them.

This change in the balance of power caused some rapid developments in the Orkneys. Brusi had died and the ever-ambitious Thorfinn now took control of the entire jarldom, including Caithness and Sutherland and the Hebrides. According to the saga writer:

Jarl Thorfinn became a great chief. He was the tallest and strongest of men, with black hair, sharp features, and a somewhat swarthy countenance. He was a man of great energy and greedy for wealth and honour. He was lucky in battle, skilled in the art of war, and dauntless in courage.

For a few years Thorfinn had absolute control over the Orkneys but then, in 1037, the Norwegian court discovered Olaf's claim and demanded the same feudal rights. At Magnus' court, Rognvald Brussisson had developed into a fine warrior. Rognvald had accompanied Olaf when he fled into exile at Kiev and returned with him to fight at Stiklestad. After Olaf's death Rognvald carried the wounded body of Harald Sigurdsson, Olaf's half-brother, from the battlefield, following the survivors back to Russia. A saga writer comments:

> Eager for battle
> A war-god he grew;
> Ten shower of the shield file
> Fought he in Russia.

Rognvald Brussisson was certainly a favourite of the new Norwegian monarch and, on discovering Norway's claim to the Orkneys, Magnus sent him to obtain suzerainty over the jarldom. As Brusi's son, Rognvald claimed a third share of the jarldom as well. One third was to be Thorfinn's, one third Rognvald's, and one third was to go to Magnus, who expected acknowledgment as overlord of the jarldom. Naturally Thorfinn was angered at this turn of events. But the *Orkneyinga Saga* explains:

> At that moment Jarl Thorfinn had his hands full with the men of the Hebrides and the Irish and he felt himself much in need of help in the way of forces. And he made the answer to Rognvald's envoys that he may take under his rule the land of the islands which is his right.

Although thrown together in this somewhat inauspicious way, Thorfinn and his nephew, Rognvald, seemed to get on well enough initially. In the spring of 1039 it is recorded that they went on a war cruise together around the Hebrides, Ireland and along the west coast of Scotland. Arnor, Thorfinn's skald, went with them and records one battle between the Norsemen and some Scottish clans at a place he names as Loch Vatten:

> Deeds done doughtily
> By my lord at Loch Vatten
> By the Tester of Men;
> — I was with him in peril.
> Swiftly the warrior band
> Bore up the shield wall...
> The grey wolf was gaping
> Over each bloody corpse.

The deeds of Thorfinn and Rognvald won them both honour and respect among the Norsemen. When they finally quarrelled, Arnor underlined the sadness and confusion of the men of Orkney at having to choose between them. Arnor also gives us significant insight into the extent of Thorfinn's ambitions:

> The Man of the Sword,
> Seeking Scotland's throne,
> Ever won victory.
> Fire flamed fiercely,
> Fast fell the Irish host
> And flower of Welsh manhood.

Scotland thus lay between two ambitious men. In the north was Malcolm II's grandson, Thorfinn, ruthless and efficient. In the south, at Scone, was another grandson, Duncan, now the High King, ambitious but, as time would show, weak and incompetent. And between the two stood a third grandson of Malcolm II, MacBeth, the Mormaer of Moray.

CHAPTER FIVE

'Hard steel swung
In dark Scottish blood...'

Arnor the Skald

In 1040 MacBeth Mac Findlaech, Mormaer of Moray, overthrew the High King, Duncan Mac Crinan, who was slain in battle at Burghead in Moray. MacBeth was then acclaimed High King of Scotland and thus was created the basis of one of history's greatest myths – the murder of Duncan by MacBeth as set out in Shakespeare's play. Nothing could be further from the truth than Shakespeare's account. The overthrow of Duncan was the overthrow of an unpopular king who was intent on pursuing an aggressive, expansionist war against England and, at the same time, against the Orkney jarldom – a war in which he soon showed himself to be militarily incompetent and therefore incompetent to retain the High Kingship to which he had been elected.

Duncan was far from 'the gracious king' of the play. Andrew of Wyntoun, in *The Orygynale Cronykil of Scotland*, tells us that Duncan was a vicious, bloodthirsty, selfish tyrant who satisfied his lusts in the most unscrupulous way. We can assume that this was a fairly conservative view of Duncan, for Wyntoun is not overzealous in exaggerating the virtues of MacBeth. And certainly, when Duncan was killed, no contemporary chronicler raised a voice in protest. The general consensus of opinion was that Scotland had changed its ruler for the better. It was not until three centuries later that historians began to use the terms 'usurpation' and 'murder'.

How had Duncan's overthrow, with the popular support of the

Scottish people, been possible? The answer seems to lie in Duncan's greed, ambition and incompetence. He probably aspired to live up to his grandfather's image. Malcolm had united the country under a strong rule for thirty years. He had repelled Danish imperial excursions and had annexed the territory of Bernica. His ambition was matched by his strength and ability. If Malcolm II was not liked by the Scottish people, especially the northern clans of Moray, he was, at least, respected as a competent High King.

The first test of Duncan's ability as a leader came in 1038 when the Earl of Northumbria, Eadulf, son of Earl Uchtred, marched against the southern Scottish provinces. The purpose appears to have been to win back the Bernican territory which Malcolm had annexed in 1018. The Northumbrians ravaged Cumbria, but Maldred, Duncan's brother, who now ruled as provincial king there, managed to repulse them.

After this attack Duncan must have come under pressure from his mormaers and chieftains to retaliate, which would, in any case, have coincided with his own plans to extend the borders of Scotland. He could either march south, across the River Tweed and on towards Durham, or he could go north, take Caithness and Sutherland, unite all the mainland under his rule and, perhaps, force Thorfinn to acknowledge the suzerainty of Scone over all the Orkney jarldom. Duncan's incompetence and foolhardiness as a military leader is demonstrated by the fact that he chose to push on both fronts at the same time and it was this that ultimately led to his downfall.

In choosing the spring or early summer of the year 1040 as the time to begin his expansion into England, Duncan did, at least, choose the most opportune moment. On 17 March Harald Harefoot, the King of England, died at Oxford after a long illness. He was about twenty-six years old. His brother, Hardicanute, who had considered himself the legitimate heir and successor to Canute, had been preparing to invade the country with a Danish army to enforce his claim. He landed at Sandwich in midsummer and, shortly afterwards, was crowned at Canterbury. But between the death of Harald Harefoot and the arrival of Hardicanute, England had been thrown into chaos.

When Canute died in 1035 he had designated Hardicanute as

his successor but Harald had taken advantage of Hardicanute's absence from the country to have himself nominated king by the English parliament. The most powerful of the English provincial rulers, Earl Godwin of Wessex, declared for Hardicanute. But Wessex stood alone. Earl Leofric of Mercia, husband of Lady Godiva, took up Harald Harefoot's cause and was supported by Eadulf of Northumbria. London, then a thriving Danish colony, also declared for Harald. Godwin's only support came from Emma, Hardicanute's mother, who promptly declared herself regent. Protected by Godwin, she established a court at Winchester in Hardicanute's name.

Civil war was imminent but Godwin eventually recognized Harald as king. It was an uneasy peace. An attempt to seize the crown was suddenly made, not by Hardicanute, but by Emma's sons by her first marriage to Ethelred. These were Alfred and Edward Aetheling who had grown to manhood at the court of their kinsman, the Duke of Normandy. Edward Aetheling sailed from Normandy with a fleet of forty ships, landed near Southampton and marched to his mother's court at Winchester. Emma, his mother, refused to acknowledge him and eventually the young man had to flee back to Normandy. His brother, Alfred Aetheling, also came to England, probably at the invitation of the devious Earl Godwin, who promised him aid in securing the throne for the Anglo-Saxon dynasty. He was met at Guildford by Godwin. During the night Alfred and his party were seized, some were slain and others sold as slaves. Alfred was taken before Harald Harefoot in London. It was rumoured that Godwin did this to regain favour with Harald, who ordered the Anglo-Saxon prince to be blinded, which was done with such savagery that the young man died soon after in prison at Ely.

At last, after a short reign noted for its barbarity, Harald Harefoot died. He left a great personal fortune which had been amassed by the selling of Church preferments. England was once again in turmoil over who should succeed to the throne – would it be Hardicanute, preparing his invasion of England with the aid of Baldwin of Flanders, or Edward Aetheling, in exile in Normandy? This was how matters stood when the High King of Scotland led his army into Northumbria.

Duncan was not the only neighbouring monarch to seize on

England's misfortunes. The pugnacious Welsh ruler, Gruffydd ap Llewelyn ap Seisyll, who had become King of Gwynnedd in 1039, had already, in 1040, seized the opportunity to invade and plunder Leofric's earldom of Mercia. The author of *Brut y Twysogion* (Chronicle of the Welsh Princes) records of Gruffydd's career, 'From the beginning to the end, he hounded the pagans and Saxons in many battles, and he prevailed against them and slaughtered and ravaged them'. His invasion of the Mercian earldom was successful and bloody. Leofric's own brother, Edwin, and many other English nobles were killed in Gruffydd's invasion. It may well have been this success that inspired Duncan in his march into Northumbria.

Perhaps if Duncan had committed all his army to his invasion of England a different story would have been told. But he did not. Before marching his main body of clansmen to the south, he sent a peremptory message to Thorfinn Sigurdsson. The *Orkneyinga Saga* briefly states: 'Jarl Hundi's son then succeeded to the Scottish realm. He thought he ought to own Caithness as well as the former Scottish kings.' Duncan's demand was that, as Malcolm II had bestowed the title of 'Jarl of Caithness' on Thorfinn when he was five years old, and that as Thorfinn had initially recognized the suzerainty of Scone over the Orkneys, Thorfinn should now recognize the right of Duncan to be High King over the territory. Thorfinn regarded Caithness as a personal gift and the jarls of the Orkneys had long laid claim to the territory. It was not likely that he was going meekly to pay Duncan tribute or give up the territory to him. His reply, if he sent one, is not recorded.

Duncan then provocatively named his nephew, Moddan, as ruler of Caithness and ordered the young man to march northward with a force of Atholl clansmen to assert his rights by force. Without waiting to hear the outcome, Duncan then marched his own army into Northumbria.

It would appear that Duncan's immediate plan was to seize the city of Durham, populous and well-fortified, second only to York as the most important centre in the Northumbrian earldom. The only suffragan to the bishopric of York was based in Durham, and the city was crowned by a splendid minster. It was a prominent market and trading centre. If this walled city fell to

Duncan, it would be of great strategic value and give Duncan's troops confidence enough to march on York, the most important city in the north of England. Remembering that the southern border of Scotland was the Cumbrian border, it could be that Duncan's ambitious plan was to extend that border from Morecambe Bay on the west coast to the River Humber on the east. If so, it was an ambitious plan.

But Duncan's generalship against Durham soon revealed his military incompetence. It appears that he flung his cavalry against the fortified walls of the city. Its historian, Symeon of Durham, records that large sections of the Scottish cavalry were simply annihilated as they tried to breach the walls. With the Scottish cavalry severely mauled, the Northumbrians came out of the city and counter-attacked. Duncan lost nearly all his foot-soldiers. The Scots panicked and fled. It is recorded that the Northumbrians collected the heads of all the slain Scottish troops and placed them on posts in the city's market place as grisly trophies of their victory. Duncan fell back on Berwick-on-Tweed, bitter in defeat.

While resting there he was confronted by the bedraggled figure of his nephew, Moddan, who arrived with more humiliating news for the High King. Moddan had marched confidently northwards with his clansmen. On his arrival at the borders of Caithness and Sutherland, he learnt that Thorfinn Sigurdsson was prepared for him. A large army of Orkneymen, under the command of Thorfinn and Thorkell Fosterer, had been assembled. Moddan, perhaps wisely, had retreated without penetrating any further into Caithness. For a while the Norse army pursued him.

Duncan was not pleased with Moddan's story, especially coming so soon after his own ignominious defeat. He decided, therefore, to do what a good military commander would have done in the first place – to concentrate all his forces on one enemy. He decided to try and subdue Thorfinn first. A new and larger army was to be gathered by Moddan and marched overland to Caithness. Duncan himself would gather a further force of men and transport them in eleven warships from Berwick and land them on the northern coast of Caithness, thus placing Thorfinn's army between the two armies of the Scottish clansmen.

47

However, Duncan was dealing with an astute general in the Jarl of the Orkneys. Thorfinn had already sent Thorkell Fosterer and his main army back to the Orkneys and, aware that Duncan would not let the matter rest, was waiting with five longboats off Duncansby Head in Caithness in case of a seaborne invasion of his jarldom. Meanwhile, Duncan sailed northwards while Moddan marched his clansmen overland once more.

The author of the *Orkneyinga Saga* pays tribute to Duncan for his enterprise:

> Now it must be told of Jarl Hundi's son that he never shortened sail 'til he got to Caithness: and there was but a little distance between him and Thorfinn. Thorfinn at that moment decided to board ship, hold out to Pentland Firth, and make for the Orkneys. But, by that time, so short was the distance between them, that Jarl Hundi's son and his men spied Thorfinn's sails as he sailed east into the Firth. And they at once sailed after him.

Thorfinn, obviously thinking that Duncan was not coming, had decided to make for Sandwick in the Orkneys. On spotting Duncan's larger fleet, he 'ran in under Deerness from the east, and at once sent a message to Thorkell to muster an army.'

Thorfinn and his five longboats arrived off Deerness at night and when the sun rose the next morning he saw that Duncan's men were rowing their warships up to his. Thorfinn had two courses open to him. He could beach his ships under Deerness and take to the land with his men, leaving his ships and belongings to Duncan as spoils of war. Or he could take the offensive.

Thorfinn took the second course and ordered his warships to row against Duncan's ships. 'This battle was hard and prolonged,' says the writer of the *Orkneyinga Saga*, 'and for long it was not clear on which side the scale would fall.' Arnor, Thorfinn's skald, described the battle in the traditional manner:

> East of Deerness
> Our hero fought Jarl Hundi's son,
> The mail coat's strong judgement;
> Safe were the prince's lands,
> Steadfast in anger,
> Flight scorning, the mighty man,

Advanced on the High King
Five ships to eleven.

The ships drove alongside,
On the decks dropped the host,
Hard steel swung
In dark Scottish blood.
Our prince was stout-hearted.
Bow sang, steel bit,
Blood flowed, shafts flew,
Spear-point glittered.

The *Orkneyinga Saga* records:

Then he laid his ship alongside Jarl Hundi's son's ship; and then came the stiffest fighting of all. The Scots bunched together on the High King's ship just before the mast. And then Jarl Thorfinn leaps off the poop, forward into the High King's ship, and lays about him boldly. When he saw that the numbers were thinning on the High King's ship, he called on his men to come aboard. And when King Duncan saw that, he gave orders to cut the lashings (get all the fleet under weigh, take to the oars) and stand off to sea.

In response to Duncan's attempt to disengage, Thorfinn ordered more grappling lines to be anchored to the High King's boat. With a warrior carrying the famous 'raven banner' before him, Thorfinn and his Orkneymen fought along the entire length of Duncan's ship. Duncan, seeing his own capture imminent, leapt from his ship with those men who remained unwounded, although we are told by the *Saga*'s author that 'most of the band had fallen in that ship'. Duncan managed to climb aboard another Scottish ship and ordered it to disengage at once.

Thorfinn returned to his own longboat and had the derelict Scottish vessel cut away. He then set off in pursuit of the fleeing Scottish fleet. Arnor rhapsodized:

Shooting of spears made
Long battle thunder.
Thy mighty lord routed
His mightiest foe.
Screamed high the battle-bird
Reddened our hands in blood.
Won was the victory,
South of Sandwick.

Duncan's ships fled back into the Pentland Firth and turned south towards Moray Firth. The exuberant Thorfinn met up with Thorkell Fosterer's fleet, hastening from the Orkneys to his aid. The two forces pursued Duncan into the Moray Firth where the High King landed. The *Orkneyinga Saga* says that Duncan 'went ashore there, and mustered a fresh force'. No other details are known.

The Orkney fleets began to harry the coastal settlements of Moray and, while they were thus engaged, news reached Thorfinn that Moddan had arrived in Caithness with his army. Moddan's Atholl clansmen were apparently not a large force and had encamped in the Norse settlement of Thjórsá or Thurso – Bull's Water. They were apparently awaiting reinforcement by a contingent of Irish levies. It is interesting to note that Duncan could claim the allegiance of Irish warriors. It could be that the Scottish High Kings had a right to command their allegiance for St Berchan speaks of Duncan's grandfather, Malcolm II, as 'son of the woman of Leinster'. It would seem that Malcolm II's mother was related to the rulers of Leinster and it could be that this family connection helped Duncan to obtain the services of Irish levies or, alternatively, Duncan may have asked the Irish to repay an old obligation, pointing out that when the High King of Ireland, Brían Boru had asked for Scottish troops to help him drive back the Norse invaders into the sea at Clontarf in 1014, Scotland had willingly sent troops. Now Duncan was asking for help to drive Thorfinn out of Scotland. But it must also be remembered that the employment of a mercenary force was fairly common during this period and, especially among the Celtic lands, we find bands of Celts fighting in wars clearly not their own. The appearance of Irish troops fighting for the High King of Scotland was no more unusual than it was to find Welsh bowmen fighting for the Irish, or Bretons for the Cornish. The Celts, at this time, still moved freely through each other's countries as they had in ancient times when the druidic order provided a bond of unity between all Celtic countries. Now the Celtic Christian Church had replaced the druidic order as the symbol of such unity. There is one significant fact which must be emphasized: the prominence of the Irish troops serving Duncan suggests that the High King was not able to rely entirely on his Scottish clansmen.

When Thorfinn Sigurdsson heard that Moddan and his clansmen were camped at Thurso he split his force and sent a detachment of men under Thorkell Fosterer to deal with them. Thorkell landed on the south-eastern coast of Caithness and made a rapid march overland to Thurso, for, says the *Orkneyinga Saga*, 'All the common folk of Caithness were trusty and true to him. No word of his journey got before him until he entered Thurso at dead of night.'

The Norsemen surprised the clansmen in their sleep and the Scots were either killed or taken prisoner. Moddan was sleeping in the upper room of a house in Thurso which was surrounded by Thorkell's men and set on fire. 'Just as he leapt over the balcony, Thorkell hewed at him and struck his neck and took off his head.' Moddan and his army thus destroyed, Thorkell rejoined Thorfinn on the 'north coast of Moray and told him how his errand had sped'.

Thorfinn was based at Burghead where his father Sigurd had built a *borg* or fortress from which the modern township takes its name. This enabled the Norsemen to maintain a footing in the area. They apparently called the area Torfness, although some scholars are inclined to think that this is synonymous with Tarbat Ness to the north, between Dornoch Firth and Moray Firth. According to the *Orkneyinga Saga* Duncan had 'sent far and wide to chiefs for forces' and now had a sizeable army, perhaps some 5,000 to 10,000 men, to face Thorfinn. The *Saga* says that the Scottish clansmen came 'as well as from the south as the west and east of Scotland and all the way from Satiri and Kintyre, and the force for which Jarl Moddan had sent also came to him from Ireland'. It is significant, as we shall later see, that the *Saga* makes no mention of a force coming from the northern province of Scotland – Moray.

On Thursday, 14 August, 1040, the day before the Feast of the Assumption, the forces of Duncan Mac Crinan, High King of Scotland, clashed with those of Thorfinn Sigurdsson, Jarl of the Orkneys. The *Orkneyinga Saga* records:

> Jarl Thorfinn was in the van of his troops; he had a gilded helmet on his head, he was girt with a sword, and he had a great spear in his hand which he wielded to right and left.

Thorfinn took the initiative by opening the battle with a fierce attack on the Irish levies. The *Saga* says that the Irish were quickly routed. The Celts, in general, preferred to fight without the cumbersome body armour which the Norsemen wore. In this way they could move about more easily but, on the other hand, when pressed in close formation by a phalanx of determined, well-armoured warriors, they were totally vulnerable. Over a century later, when the Normans invaded Ireland, the Irish were to fall easy victims to the armoured knights. The superiority of the Norse weapons – the heavy swords, iron spears, helmets and mail armour – always put the Celts at a disadvantage, though the Celts did eventually learn from the Norsemen how to use weapons such as the claymore (*claidh mhór*, or great sword), a two-handed, double-edged longsword. Today the term claymore is inaccurately applied to a one-handed, basket-hilted sword.

Thorfinn's skald, Arnor, who mistakenly records that the battle was fought on a Monday, enthused:

> A keen sword at Torfness
> Reddened the wolf's fame.
> The young prince wielded it.
> It was a Monday.
> This sword sang there,
> South off Oykell.
> They fought, the Scottish King
> And our valiant lord.
>
> After the crashing of spears
> Orkney's lord in the van
> Bore high his helm;
> Exulted in battle,
> He reddened Irish blood,
> Spear point and sword edge,
> Stout arm at onset,
> Kinsman of Hlodver,
> This gracious lord of mine,
> Raising his Welsh shield,
> Rushed upon the host.

In spite of the rout of the Irish levies, Duncan managed to organize a counter-attack. The Scottish clansmen rushed down on Thorfinn's centre, only to be repulsed. The *Orkneyinga Saga* rounds off the battle by saying, 'But it ended in the flight of the King, and some say he was slain'.

It is the Benedictine monk from Donegal, Muiredach Mac Robertaigh, better known as Marianus Scotus, who confirms what the author of the *Orkneyinga Saga* leaves to hearsay. He writes in his *Chronicon Universal* that 'Duncan, High King of Scotland was slain on August 14 by his general, MacBeth, son of Finlay'. This is the first time that the Mormaer of Moray is mentioned in the war between Duncan and Thorfinn. Throughout the *Orkneyinga Saga* there is no mention of MacBeth. Another contemporary chronicler, Tighernach O'Braein, says that 'Duncan Mac Crinan, High King of Scotland, was slain by his own subjects at an immature age'. As regards age, Tighernach is wrong because Duncan was thirty-nine years old when he died. But we are left with the two separate and fairly contemporary sources stating that Duncan was killed by his own men, one of these sources specifically naming MacBeth.

As Marianus Scotus, writing some twenty or thirty years after the event, is the only contemporary writer who names MacBeth as the general of Duncan's army as well as his slayer, we must ask ourselves to what extent we can rely on Marianus' report in the absence of any confirmation.

There are two possibilities. First that Marianus Scotus is right and that MacBeth was indeed the commander of the army of Duncan, High King of Scotland. The second possibility is that Marianus Scotus is wrong and that MacBeth had, throughout the conflict between Duncan and Thorfinn, supported the Jarl of the Orkneys. If we assume that Marianus Scotus was right, MacBeth and the clans of Moray would have rallied to Duncan's standard when he landed on the shores of Moray Firth, after fleeing from Thorfinn at Deerness, a refugee with few followers. As Duncan's cousin and also the provincial ruler, MacBeth would naturally assume the position of commander of the new forces raised in his province. This would fit in with the *Orkneyinga Saga*'s report that when Duncan got to Moray Firth he 'went ashore there and mustered a fresh force'. But the *Saga* also says that Duncan 'sent far and wide to chiefs for forces' and mentions troops 'from the south', also from 'the west and the east of Scotland', even from Kintyre. The north, Moray, is not mentioned.

My contention is that Marianus Scotus was wrong, that circumstances prohibited MacBeth from becoming Duncan's commander. I further believe that subsequent events, such as the amicable relationship between MacBeth and Thorfinn, confirm this interpretation.

Let us remember that when Duncan landed on the coast of Moray he was fleeing from a disastrous defeat at the hands of Thorfinn. Earlier he had been forced to flee from another such defeat at the hands of the English and, at the same time, his nephew, Moddan, had fled before Thorfinn without attempting to do battle. Soon after Duncan's arrival in Moray came the news of the slaughter of Moddan and his clansmen at Thurso. Duncan's reputation in the eyes of the Scottish people could not have been very high at that time.

In Celtic law, it must be remembered, the office of High King was elective, rather like the president of a modern-day republic, and if he did not promote the welfare of the people he was soon deposed. Duncan's territorial ambitions had led Scotland into a war of expansion both to the south and to the north, in the course of which he had suffered four defeats in rapid succession. The evidence of early chroniclers is that Duncan was not a popular ruler and had been proved incompetent in his handling of military affairs. That fact, coupled with the long rivalry between Moray and Atholl, make it quite feasible that the clansmen of Moray rose up against the High King and slew him, and quite possibly that MacBeth himself executed the deed. But it is entirely inconsistent with the evidence that MacBeth could have been in command of Duncan's army against Thorfinn.

It has already been noted that there was an intense rivalry between the Houses of Atholl and Moray, that political power in Scotland was divided between the two and that the High Kingship was a constant source of conflict between them. It has also been shown that Malcolm II, in order to secure Duncan's succession to the High Kingship, annihilated the most likely candidates of the Moray faction. Gillecomgain, a cousin of MacBeth, had been burnt alive in his fortress; Malcolm Mac Bodhe, grandson of Kenneth III and brother of MacBeth's wife, had been murdered in 1033; Gruoch, the granddaughter of Kenneth III, and her son, Lulach, had barely escaped with their lives when Gillecomgain, her first husband, was slain. The fact that MacBeth, on his election as Mormaer of Moray, married Gruoch and adopted Lulach must have been seen as an insult by Duncan. Duncan might well call himself *Ard Righ na h-Alba* (High King of Scotland) in Scone but north of the Mounth Mountains his rule was not really valid and the Mormaers of Moray were still referred to by contemporary chroniclers as *Righ na h-Alba* (Kings of Scotland).

Would MacBeth have raised the clans of Moray to support the head of the House of Atholl, albeit his own cousin? It must be remembered that Thorfinn Sigurdsson was also MacBeth's cousin and there is no record of any recent conflict between Moray and the Jarl of the Orkneys, while there are records of raids by the Moraymen against Atholl. Would the Moray clansmen have come out to defend Duncan whose House of Atholl had been responsible for the raids and massacres which were all part of Malcolm's and Duncan's sustained campaign to weaken the northern clans and make them submit to the will of Scone?

It is not only on this basis that I believe MacBeth and the Moray clans did not fight for Duncan. There is also the fact that Thorfinn totally defeated Duncan's army and chased it as far south as Fife. If MacBeth had been the 'enemy general', why did Thorfinn let him go south to Scone and claim the High Kingship when he, also a grandson of Malcolm II, might easily have made a similar claim? Arnor wrote that Thorfinn was 'seeking Scotland's throne'; and there would never have been a better opportunity. But Thorfinn was content to return to the Orkneys. Why? My contention is that MacBeth not only did *not* fight for Duncan but that he formed an alliance with his cousin Thorfinn to depose the King.

MacBeth must have realized that if Duncan succeeded in destroying the power of Thorfinn, then Duncan's own power would be absolute and he would take the first opportunity to finish the job he and his grandfather, Malcolm, had begun – to crush for ever the power of Moray. It would be logical, therefore, that if Moray was to survive then Thorfinn Sigurdsson must also survive. On this basis MacBeth would have formed an alliance with Thorfinn. This alliance, I believe, is confirmed by the fact that MacBeth and Thorfinn divided the spoils between them after

Duncan's defeat: MacBeth became High King and Thorfinn was confirmed in his jarldom and given other territories by MacBeth. The *Orkneyinga Saga* boasts that Thorfinn had 'nine earldoms in Scotland, the whole of the Hebrides and a large *riki* (estate) in Ireland'.

If MacBeth had been commander of Duncan's defeated army, even though he had turned on the High King and slain him, Thorfinn, as the victorious commander, would not meekly have allowed MacBeth to keep all Scotland for himself. Thorfinn was as ambitious to extend his domains as his grandfather had been. So the division seems to bear out my contention that a clear agreement was made between Thorfinn and MacBeth before the battle at Burghead, and that the Moray clansmen played a decisive role in the defeat of the unpopular High King.

Duncan was slain at Pitgaveny, two miles north-east of Elgin. The first reference to his having been murdered rather than killed in battle does not occur until some 350 years after the event. The site of Duncan's death is given in the *Register of St Andrews* which records: *'Doncath interfectus est in Bothgouan'*. Bothgouan or Both na Gobhainn – the cabin of the blacksmith – became anglicized over the years to Pitgowney and then Pitgaveny. There is another site in the vicinity where tradition has it that Duncan, fleeing from the disaster at Burghead, was overtaken and cut down by MacBeth's men. This is a standing stone in the parish of Duffus, some three and a half miles south-east of Burghead and just north of Elgin. But all the earliest sources are agreed that Both na Gobhainn is the site of Duncan's death.

The myth of Duncan's murder at Cawdor Castle was created many centuries afterwards. Visitors of a morbid curiosity are conducted to a room in Cawdor Castle called King Duncan's Room, to be shown a brown stain on its floor, while a guide pronounces that they are looking at 'Duncan's blood' in the very room where the so-called murder was carried out. The only thing wrong with the legend, apart from the site being a long way from Both na Gobhainn, is that Cawdor Castle was not built until 400 years after the death of Duncan!

Duncan, therefore, having witnessed the disintegration of his Irish levies and the repulse of his own clansmen, fled from the field of Burghead in the direction of Elgin. It was his fifth and final defeat during that short summer of 1040. He was pursued by Thorfinn and MacBeth. They, or their men, caught up with him at a blacksmith's cottage near Elgin and slew him. John of Fordun says that Duncan was only wounded but conveyed to Elgin where he died.

The *Orkneyinga Saga* says that Thorfinn drove the rest of Duncan's army clear down into Fife where they were eventually subdued. But, according to the *Saga*, it took a long while for the Scottish clansmen to make a total submission, and certainly, as they neared their own clan lands to the south, the men of Duncan's army would have stiffened their resistance. The author of the *Saga* records:

> Some of those very men who submitted to him (Thorfinn) marched against him (again). And as soon as the jarl got word of their treachery he called together his forces and marched to meet them. The Scots were less anxious to rebel when they learnt the jarl was ready for them. As soon as he came near the Scots, Jarl Thorfinn prepared for battle, but they took to flight and scattered in all directions to the woods and thickets. And after the jarl had pursued them he called in all his army, and says that he will have the whole province burned in which they then were and pay the Scots out for their enmity and treachery.

Thorfinn was certainly in no mood to show leniency. The *Saga* tells us that the Orkneymen went round every village and township in the province (Fife) 'and burned right and left so that not a cottage was left standing'. They killed all the men who had taken arms against them, while the women and old men took themselves off to the woods and hills to hide until the rampaging Norsemen had gone. Even so, the *Saga* records that they took many captives, putting them in fetters and driving them before them. Arnor praises the day's work:

> Humbled the homesteads
> Burning in Scotland.
> Red flame from smoking thatch
> Shot high; for that day
> Dire danger failed not.
> Vengeance for broken word
> Tried warriors ever give
> Thrice ere the fall of beat
> Triumphed over chieftain.

Thorfinn's ruthlessness and the remarks of Arnor about a 'broken word' would indicate that the remnants of Duncan's army had initially made terms with Thorfinn and then betrayed those terms by attacking him. This offers further proof that MacBeth could not have been in command of Duncan's men. It also makes it more likely that MacBeth and Thorfinn were allies. Once again it must be observed that Thorfinn, according to Arnor, wanted the throne of Scotland for himself and his ruthlessness demonstrates that he had no feelings of faint-heartedness about taking what he wanted. Were MacBeth the defeated enemy commander who had turned on his own king and slain him to curry favour with the conquering Norse jarl, then Thorfinn certainly would not have turned quietly back to the Orkneys, leaving the High Kingship he coveted and the rich, unplundered southern lands of Scotland to MacBeth.

But Thorfinn did withdraw to the Orkneys and left his thirty-five-year-old cousin, MacBeth Mac Findlaech, to continue his march to Scone and lay his claim before the assembled mormaers, chieftains and churchmen of Scotland.

CHAPTER SIX

'Brimful of food was Scotland, east and west,
During the reign of the ruddy, brave king.'

St Berchan

In the summer of 1040 two kings were crowned in Britain. At Canterbury, Hardicanute, the last of the Danish royal dynasty in England, was crowned King. At Scone, MacBeth Mac Findlaech was crowned *Ard Righ na h-Alba*, High King of Scotland. Of the two nations it was the English who were to suffer from the murderous whims of a petty despot, but, ironically, it was the Scottish ruler who was to be immortalized in that role.

While Thorfinn, MacBeth and Duncan had been fighting at Burghead, Hardicanute had landed at Sandwich with a formidable armada of sixty warships. Soon afterwards he was crowned at Canterbury and accepted by the Witenagemot. He began his reign with a disgraceful act of petty vengeance: he ordered the body of his brother, Harald Harefoot, to be taken from its tomb at Westminster, beheaded and thrown into the Thames. MacBeth, on the other hand, allowed the body of Duncan to be escorted to the isle of Iona where it was laid to rest in the graveyard of all lawful Scottish kings.

Hardicanute continued his despotic rule by levying heavy taxes to pay for his Danish army. A sum of £22,000 was levied in the first year, and £11,000 in the next – considerable sums for those days. When the city of Worcester refused to pay the tax, an army, led by Earl Leofric of Mercia and the Danish noble, Siward, was sent against the city which was razed to the ground after five days of bitter fighting. Many of the citizens escaped only to be cut down by Hardicanute's troops while trying to defend themselves on a tiny island in the Severn estuary. Hardicanute's army spent most of its time acting as tax-collectors for their rapacious new King. Legend has it that Earl Leofric's wife, Lady Godiva, rode naked through the streets of Coventry to shame her husband into preventing the imposition of these taxes.

Hardicanute tried to destroy the power of Earl Godwin of Wessex and had the Witenagemot accuse him of the murder of Alfred Aetheling. Godwin was tried by the nobles and churchmen of England but, by careful bribes, such as the gift of a splendid ship to Hardicanute, he procured his acquittal. Godwin's ship caused much comment and Florence of Worcester has left an enthusiastic description of it. He says it had a gilded beak, was equipped in a most perfect manner, with eighty warriors to man it. Every warrior bore a gold bracelet of sixteen ounces in weight on each arm; they were each armed with a strongly woven habergon, or sleeveless coat of mail, and a helmet partly made of gilt. Each was armed with a sword, while from the left shoulder hung a Danish axe bound with gold and silver; in the left hand they carried a shield, the boss and nails of which were gilded, and in the right hand a lance.

England groaned under the reign of Hardicanute until 8 June, 1042. On that day he attended the wedding feast of a Danish noble called Tofig, who was his standard bearer. Tofig was marrying the daughter of another Danish noble named Clapa, from whom the London suburb of Clapham takes its name. According to the *Anglo-Saxon Chronicle*, Hardicanute 'was standing at his drink and suddenly fell to the ground with fearful convulsions and those who were near him caught him and he spoke no words afterwards'. The last Danish king of England was dead. He was in his twenty-third or twenty-fourth year. The cause of death was either an epileptic fit or poison. Edward Aetheling was now invited by the Witenagemot to resume the interrupted Anglo-Saxon dynasty.

In the meantime Scotland enjoyed the rule of he whom St Berchan described as the 'liberal king'. The *Chronica de Mailros* said 'MacBeth became King of Scotland for seventeen years and in his reign there were productive seasons.' Even later historians like Wyntoun, writing 350 years after MacBeth's death, recorded that:

All hys tyme wes gret plente
Abowndand bath in land and see,
He wes in justice rycht lawfull.

All his time was great plenty
Abounding both on land and sea.
He was in justice right lawful.

MacBeth probably arrived at Scone in late August, 1040, and the news of Duncan's defeat and death must have preceded him. Scone, or Sgàin – the rent or chasm, was a considerable city, as befitted the capital of the country. Constantine MacBeth (900–942) was commonly said to have been the first High King to have been crowned there, although Kenneth Mac Alpin had earlier made it his capital. Certainly as early as 906 documents refer to Scone as 'the royal city' and mention is made of a palatial *bruigheann* (royal residence).

Before MacBeth could be acclaimed High King a council of Scottish leaders would have been convened to debate his claim. Also given a voice in this election were the church leaders, such as the primate of Scotland, Maelduin Mac Gille Odrain, the Bishop of St Andrews. Should they make a wrong decision they, in turn, were answerable to the people who elected them. The law tract called the *Crith Gablach* significantly points out: 'What makes the King higher than the people? Because it is the people that ordains the King, not the King that ordains the people.' The concept of the 'divine right of kings', propounded by the anglicized Stuart monarchy of Scotland and later of England, would have been totally incomprehensible in Scotland in the eleventh century.

Several days were probably spent in council while MacBeth's claim – his lineage and his ability to govern – were discussed. We can assume that Duncan's father, Crinan, the Abbot of Dunkeld and Mormaer of Atholl, led the opposition at these meetings. But could the House of Atholl put forward a suitable alternative to the Mormaer of Moray? Was Duncan's brother, Maldred, the petty ruler of Cumbria, still alive? If so, he could well have been a candidate. If not, was Gospadruig, Maldred's son, who later called himself King of Cumbria, qualified to stand? Under Celtic law, Duncan's three children by his Danish wife were not eligible

61

to be considered for the office as they were all under age. Eventually the assembled chieftains and churchmen of Scotland decided for MacBeth and he was dúly crowned at Scone.

After the consecration by the Bishop of St Andrews, MacBeth, like Scottish kings before and after him, was led to the ancient stone known as the *Lia Fáil*, the Stone of Destiny. On this stone he would swear by his honour to serve the commonweal of Scotland and defend the well-being of her people. He was then hailed by each chieftain in turn.

The *Lia Fáil* now rests in Westminster Abbey. It was once revered as Jacob's Pillow by the clans, who believed it to have been brought from the East during the Celtic migrations across Europe nearly 2,000 years before Christ. St Colm, or Columba, is said to have crowned Aidan King of Argyll on it. It was kept at Dunstaffnage in Argyll until 848 when Kenneth Mac Alpin is said to have taken it to Scone. Thereafter all the kings of Scotland were crowned on it until it was taken to Westminster Abbey by Edward I (1272–1307) during his invasion of Scotland. Every English monarch has been crowned on it since and a legend has arisen that should the stone be taken away from Westminster it will mark the end of the British monarchy.

The *Lia Fáil* was, in fact, once removed from Westminster Abbey. In 1951 it was taken away by four patriotic Scots. Its successful removal greatly delighted Scottish public opinion which had long felt that the ancient monument, plundered so long ago from their country, should be returned. Some months later the *Lia Fáil* was found wrapped in a Scottish flag in Arbroath Abbey and returned to Westminster. Another attempt to remove it from the Abbey was made in 1967.

The stone had a deep religious significance in Celtic life which goes back into pre-history. The importance of swearing an oath by a sacred stone is frequently stressed in Celtic mythology. Near St Colm's tomb in Iona there once stood the Black Stones of Iona, so called, not because of their colour, but because of the black doom that fell on anyone who dared to violate an oath sworn on them. As recently as the reign of James VI of Scotland two clans who had spent centuries in a blood feud met on Iona and solemnly pledged themselves to friendship by the sacred stones. The last of the stones disappeared over a century ago.

MacBeth, having sworn his oath on the *Lia Fáil*, was then hailed by the official court *seanchaidh*; his office is now occupied by the Lyon King-of-Arms who presides over all questions of heraldry, court precedence and custom in Scotland. The *seanchaidh* would trace, with official pomp, MacBeth's lineage through real kings and chieftains back to the mythological rulers of the Gaels, to Gàidheal Glas, son of Scota, daughter of the Pharoah Chenthres, from whom the ancient Scots maintained that they were descended.

The last time this ancient Celtic ceremony took place at a Scottish coronation was on 13 June, 1249, when Alexander III was crowned at Scone and the court *seanchaidh* is recorded as having saluted Alexander in Scottish Gaelic, 'the *materna lingua* of Scotland', and traced his descent back to Kenneth Mac Alpin.

At thirty-five MacBeth was now legally High King of Scotland. According to Mrs Stopes, in her study *The Scottish and English Macbeth*, 'In the critical state of affairs everybody seemed to think it was the best thing that could happen.' St Berchan, the Irish chronicler, was certainly in no doubt that MacBeth was a good ruler.

> ... the ruddy-faced King will possess
> the kingdom of high hilled Scotland.
> After the slaughter of the Scots, after the slaughter of the
> foreigners,
> the liberal king will possess Scotland.
> The strong one was fair, yellow haired and tall.
> Very pleasant was that handsome youth to me.
> Brimful of food was Scotland, east and west,
> During the reign of the ruddy, brave king.

The line 'After the slaughter of the Scots, after the slaughter of the foreigners' is an obvious reference to Duncan's defeat at Burghead where Scots, Irish and Norsemen were killed.

One person who saw MacBeth's succession as a tragedy was Crinan of Dunkeld. His immediate reaction was to send his three grandchildren, Duncan's sons, out of the country. The warlike Abbot probably accredited MacBeth with the same viciousness that he and his family had shown in annihilating Moray's claimants to the High Kingship, and believed that Duncan's children would be a prime target for assassination when they became old enough to challenge MacBeth under Celtic law. We know positively that the eldest son, nine-year-old Malcolm, and Domhnall Bàn (popularly anglicized as Donald Ban or Donalbain), who was seven, were sent out of the country. Their mother was a Danish noblewoman whose cousin, Siward, seized the earldom of Northumbria in 1041. Malcolm accompanied his mother to the English court, surviving the murderous reign of Hardicanute and growing up at the court of Edward the Confessor. The chroniclers make the point that, although his native speech was Gaelic, he became perfectly acquainted with Anglo-Saxon and Latin. It can also be assumed that he acquired Danish from his mother, which was used among the Danish nobility in England, and Norman-French from Edward the Confessor who spoke little Anglo-Saxon and established the language of Normandy, where he grew up in exile, as the language of the English court. Duncan's second son, Donald Ban, was sent to be fostered either in the Hebrides or in Ireland. He was given a traditional Celtic education and his knowledge of Celtic customs, law and literature was to influence his actions when he became High King in later years. Of Duncan's third son, Mael Mhuire or Melmore, there is no hint as to whether he was sent out of Scotland, but it is reasonable to believe that he was. He may well have been sent to live at the provincial court of the new Northumbrian earl, his relative Siward, for an ancient document mentions a Mael Mhuire living there. Mael Mhuire's son, Maddach, was eventually to succeed Crinan as Mormaer of Atholl and his descendants became, for a brief time, jarls of the Orkneys.

We can be sure that Crinan of Dunkeld kept in close contact with his daughter-in-law at the English court and also with Siward. His son, Maldred, and grandson, Gospadruig, would also have had close connections with Crinan and Siward and all were probably planning the overthrow of the House of Moray. However, contemporary chroniclers were already praising the wisdom of MacBeth's rule and, if MacBeth was the tyrant that Fordun speaks of over 350 years later, there is no trace of it in any contemporary account. From such sources we learn that MacBeth and Gruoch were particularly generous to the church and especially to the monastery of Loch Leven in Kinross. MacBeth granted some land in Bolgyne to the Culdees at Loch Leven 'with the utmost veneration and devotion'. Also, 'for prayers and intercessions, MacBeth son of Findlaech, and Gruoch, daughter of Bodhe, King and Queen of the Scots, granted to Almighty God and to the Culdees of the island of Loch Leven, Kirkness and its boundaries.' Kirkness lies in Portmoat near Loch Leven. These grants were recorded in the *Prioratus Sancti Andree in Scotia* (the Register of St Andrews).

Even Fordun's contemporary, Wyntoun, recorded that MacBeth made a good ruler. 'This Makbeth did many pleasand actis in the begynning of his regnne.' Hector Boece (c. 1465–1536), the friend and fellow student of Erasmus and first principal of the university at Aberdeen, mentions several specific laws that MacBeth was supposed to have enacted in his *History of Scotland*, published in Paris in 1527. Mrs Stopes, in *The Scottish and English Macbeth*, considered these laws and commented: 'I am inclined for many reasons to think there is some foundation of truth in the draft given. No one would have any interest in inventing anything that would tell in MacBeth's favour.'

Boece says that MacBeth devised an oath whereby his officers swore to defend women and orphans under the commonweal. He also claimed that MacBeth enacted a law whereby daughters could inherit as well as sons, and which specified what the dowry of a woman should be. One law Boece quotes as follows:

> Counterfeit fools, minstrels, jesters, and these kinds of jugglers, with such like idle persons that range abroad in the country having no special licence of the King, shall be compelled to learn some science or craft, to get their living by; if they refuse so to do, they shall be drawn like horses in the plough and harrows.

Boece begrudgingly admits that MacBeth's reign was wise and just, but only up to a certain date, which he gives as 1050. Then, says Boece, MacBeth became smitten by cruelty and oppression. How seriously can Boece's comments on the so-called 'laws of MacBeth' be taken? Mrs Stopes, acting more on instinct than anything else, thought they could. On turning to the Brehon Law tracts, the Celtic laws by which eleventh century Scotland was governed, the tracts list all the laws specified by Boece. Under the

Celtic law system, women held an important place compared with other civilizations. They had full right of inheritance with men, so Boece was correct in his observation that this law was current during MacBeth's reign. In Celtic law a woman remained the mistress of all she brought into a marital partnership, not only as regards her personal possessions but as regards her dowry. A woman could be elected ruler of a clan on her own merits. A traditional story from Scotland underlines the remarkable position of women at that time. The Picts were supposed, at the time the Scots were migrating from Ireland, to have had no women of child-bearing age. The Scots therefore allowed the Picts to marry Scottish women provided the succession of the Pictish kings passed through the female line. Yet another story says that the Scots stipulated that the electoral-inheritance system went through the female line because one could never be sure who one's father was but one always knew one's mother!

The law on 'counterfeit fools', which Boece quotes at length, is found exactly paralleled in an ancient Brehon tract. Boece was therefore right in suggesting that such laws applied under MacBeth's rule but wrong in attributing them to MacBeth himself. MacBeth, like all Celtic kings, was merely an officer of the established law, its administrator, and not a lawmaker, as kings were under the feudal system. The basis of the eleventh century Scottish law system was centuries old, most of the laws having their foundations in the Celtic societies which existed under the old druidic system.

For the first five years, from 1040 to 1045, MacBeth ruled a peaceful kingdom. True his cousin Thorfinn Sigurdsson had renewed his annual excursions plundering the Hebrides in 1041. This expedition affected MacBeth in that Thorfinn made landfall in the southern part of Strathclyde, known as the land of the *Gall-Ghàidheal* or 'foreign Gaels' – Galloway. Thorfinn established a camp there as a base from which to march his men into Northumbria on cattle raids. As it turned out Thorfinn was repulsed by the Northumbrians under Earl Siward. He had to retreat across the Scottish border and before he could reorganise his scattered forces winter put an end to campaigning. He returned to the Orkneys swearing vegeance. In the spring of 1042 he was ready. According to the *Orkneyinga Saga*:

Jarl Thorfinn mustered his army from the Orkneys and from Caithness and he also got large forces from Scotland and from Ireland and from all the Hebrides, men came flocking to him.

The fact that 'he also got large forces from Scotland' seems to indicate MacBeth's alliance again. Thorfinn's longboats struck first at the English coastal settlements along the west coast below Cumbria, in Leofric's earldom of Mercia. He won, according to the *Saga*, two significant battles against the Mercians before he was forced to return to the Orkneys for the winter. As always Arnor, Thorfinn's skald, vividly describes the battles:

> One battle shower
> Will the English remember;
> Never was a greater.
> There, with his warrior band,
> Came the giver of rings;
> The keen tempered sword
> Bit in the stout hearted host,
> South, off the Isle of Man,
> Rognvald the Old's son
> Fell in fight.

> Upon England's shores
> The Jarl bore his banner
> Ever and again.
> Reddening the eagle's tongue,
> The Prince bade them carry
> The Standard steadfastly.
> Flame flared,
> Roofs fell, smoke curled,
> To heaven rose the fiery gleam
> While the armed band pursued.

> Many a horn blast
> Was heard 'mid the fortresses
> Where high wind waved the banner
> Of the stout hearted prince.
> He of the open hand,
> rushed into battle.
> Now fear fell
> On the Wolf Lord's host.

In the battle at dawn
Swords were washed
And wolves tore the slain.

It would seem that MacBeth was not an 'official' ally of Thorfinn in these raids against England because contemporary chroniclers make no mention of aggressive policy by Scotland against England, nor of any retaliatory action. In all likelihood the new High King probably turned a blind eye to Thorfinn's activities in recognition of their former alliance against Duncan.

In 1045 the first and only domestic upheaval against MacBeth's rule occurred. (It must be remembered that Malcolm Canmore's overthrow of MacBeth was made with an English and Danish army and could not be described as 'domestic'.) Tighernach O'Braein and the authors of the *Annals of Ulster* and the *Annals of Loch Cé* all record that in 1045 Crinan, the Abbot of Dunkeld and Mormaer of Atholl, 'was slain and many with him. Viz. nine times twenty heroes in a battle fought between the men of Scotland at Dunkeld'.

For five years Crinan had bided his time. Then he raised some of the southern clans of Atholl against the High King. MacBeth was ready for the Hound Earl. The Atholl insurgents and the forces of the High King met at Dunkeld, fifteen miles north of Perth, on a stretch of land which rises 130 feet above sea level. The name of the settlement at this time was Dùn Chailleann, the fort of the Caledonians, from which the name Dunkeld is derived. It had once been the seat of the primacy of Scotland for here were a sixth-century church and monastery where St Colm had taught and a ninth-century church built by Kenneth Mac Alpin. The record of the engagement is brief. All that is recorded is that a battle took place here and that 180 Atholl clansmen died with their Mormaer.

After this upheaval Scotland settled back to enjoy nine more years of peace and prosperity. In fact so peaceful and secure did the kingdom become that MacBeth was able to make a pilgrimage to Rome and return to find all as he had left it.

In the years immediately following the suppression of Crinan's insurrection the events in Orkney must have caused some concern to MacBeth. For ten years Thorfinn Sigurdsson had been forced to give a third share of the jarldom to his nephew,

Rognvald Brussisson, and to acknowledge the suzerainty of Magnus, King of Norway. In 1046 he decided to break free of these constraints. His decision coincided with the arrival in the Orkneys of Kalv Arnisson, the uncle of Thorfinn's wife, Ingibjorg, who had sought Thorfinn's protection after quarrelling with Magnus. Thorfinn now made his defiance of the King of Norway an open affair by appointing Kalv ruler of the Hebrides and demanding that Rognvald leave the Orkneys.

At first Rognvald refused but Thorfinn gathered an army and he was forced to flee to Norway. Magnus immediately raised an army which, during the summer of 1046, sailed under the command of Rognvald in thirty longboats. They arrived off Roeberry, a hamlet west of St Margaret's Hope on the island of South Ronaldsay. They were met by a combined fleet commanded by Thorfinn and Kalv Arnisson, some sixty-six vessels in all, but most of them were small craft and not built for war. Rognvald, by contrast, had been provided with Norway's best warships.

It was a hard-fought battle and Arnor wrote how the Orkneymen were divided between their loyalties to Thorfinn and to Rognvald. They had served under both men and found each of them worthy of admiration.

> I beheld both my princes
> In Pentland Firth hewing
> At each other's men.
> Deep grew my sorrow,
> Blood streaked the sea,
> Blood fell on shield rim —
> Besplattered the ship —
> Black blood oozed
> From the yieldy seam.

Loyalty to Thorfinn lay deeper than loyalty to Rognvald and the Norwegian fleet was defeated. Once more Rognvald fled to Norway but he would not admit defeat. He told Magnus that he planned to return to the Orkneys immediately with one warship. 'Now when the King heard that,' says the author of the *Orkneyinga Saga*, 'he said it was folly to go before (winter was over and) the ice broken up and the sea cleared.' Rognvald was insistent:

I mean to hold west with one ship and man of it the best. Thus I expect no news of us will get there before us. Then one of two things will happen. If I reach the Isles (of Orkney) and take them by surprise, I may then win such a speedy victory as would hardly be won, if at all, with a large force. But if they are forewarned of our coming, then we can still let the sea take care of us.

Reluctantly, Magnus equipped Rognvald with a good warship and he set off at the beginning of winter, first making landfall in the Shetlands. Here he learnt that Thorfinn was on the main island of Pomona and was not expecting any further trouble until the spring. He little dreamed that Rognvald would chance the crossing in winter. Rognvald made landfall soon after dark near the place where Thorfinn was staying and surrounded the house. Thorfinn was apparently 'still sitting up drinking'. Rognvald and his men set fire to the house. According to the *Orkneyinga Saga*:

> Immediately the whole homestead blazed up. Jarl Thorfinn broke through a loft floor at the back of the house and leapt thence with his wife, Ingibjorg, in his arms. It was pitch dark and moonless and he got away through the smoke unperceived by Rognvald's men. That very night, alone in a boat, he rowed over to Caithness ... and there was no man but believed that Jarl Thorfinn had perished (in the flames).

For some weeks Thorfinn went into hiding in Caithness. In the meantime Rognvald, confident that he had killed Thorfinn, took up residence in Kirkwall. 'He had a large following,' says the *Saga*, 'and kept open house.' Thorfinn's spies watched and waited, relaying messages to the Jarl in Caithness, where he had gathered a small band of loyal men commanded by Thorkell Fosterer.

Just before the Christmas of 1046, Thorfinn's agents reported that Rognvald and some followers had gone to the island of Stronsay to collect malt for the Christmas feasts. Thorfinn and his men immediately left Caithness and sailed for Stronsay. They were able to surround and attack Rognvald's unfortified camp while he and his men were at their evening meal. Rognvald, however, managed to escape.

> They then went in search of him and split into groups, Thorkell Fosterer went along by the sea shore seeking him; and they heard a dog barking on the rocks on the shore. Jarl Rognvald had with him

his lap dog, and he gave the jarl away. They killed him there among the rocks. Some say that Thorkell Fosterer slew him because there were no other men who dared to it. He had sworn to do all those things that seemed to Thorfinn more for the safety of his realm than before.

Thorfinn then put his men aboard Rognvald's longboat and sailed it back to Kirkwall. Rognvald's followers, seeing the longboat returning, thought it was their leader and came down to the harbour to greet him. It was a matter of moments before Thorfinn's men had surrounded them and taken them prisoner. Most of them were Norwegians, members of Magnus's own bodyguard, and Thorfinn put them to death to show his contempt for the Norwegian King. Some thirty men perished in this fashion. One of them, however, Thorfinn spared and sent back to Norway to tell Magnus what had happened to Rognvald and his men and to warn him not to interfere in the affairs of the Orkney jarldom again. Rognvald's body was buried in Papa Westray.

The news of Rognvald's death did not reach Magnus until the spring of 1047 and he was 'deeply grieved at the death of his friend, Jarl Rognvald, and declared at once that he would avenge him if he got the chance'. The chance was not to come. Magnus had watched the struggle for succession in England on the death of Hardicanute with more than a passing interest. When Hardicanute had been King of Denmark, Magnus had made a treaty with him in which they agreed that when one died the survivor was to rule both Norway and Denmark. Now that Hardicanute had died in England, Magnus considered himself the legal King of Denmark. But he was immediately challenged by Hardicanute's half-brother, Sweyn, who had been left as regent in Denmark when Hardicanute went to England.

Most of the Danes supported Magnus against the tyrannical Sweyn. They wanted Magnus's military support against the Wends, a Slavic people who were harassing southern Jutland. Magnus succeeded in establishing his rule over Denmark but died soon after. The kingdoms of Norway and Denmark then fell under the rule of Harald Hardrada, who also considered himself heir to the English throne, claiming that Magnus was legally Hardicanute's heir not only to the crown of Denmark but also to the crown of England.

Thorfinn Sigurdsson sent Harald Hardrada a message of goodwill on his succession and later visited him. But Thorfinn no longer recognized the supremacy of Norway. The jarldom of the Orkneys, with the Hebrides and the territories of Caithness and Sutherland, were now an independent state. The outcome of Thorfinn's struggle must have pleased MacBeth greatly. His relationship with Thorfinn always seems to have been friendly and, had the latter been overthrown, Scotland might have found itself with an aggressive enemy on its northern and western borders.

MacBeth's Scotland now stood as an oasis of calm while internicine war raged through Norway, Denmark and England – each country interrelated in a bitter conflict which, within the next decade, was to greatly change the face of Scotland.

The crowning of a new king, Edward Aetheling, or Edward the Confessor, in England in 1043 did not stop the fighting. Edward had been 'hallowed king' at Winchester to the general delight of the English who were glad to be rid of the corrupt Danish monarchy. They saw in Edward the re-establishment of their native kings, even though Edward, brought up in Normandy, could not speak English. He was about forty years old at the time of his succession. 'A man of very comely person,' says a chronicler, 'his stature moderate; his hair and beard of singular milky whiteness; his face full, his skin rosy; his hands long and exceedingly white; his fingers long and transparent; the rest of his body without blemish; a truly kingly man.' A man almost too good to be true. But behind the façade Edward was weak and indolent, possessed of a quick temper and exaggerated piety. Edward also enjoyed vengeance. He even took his revenge against his mother, Emma of Normandy, one of his first acts being the confiscation of her property and goods in retaliation for her refusal to help him seize power when Harald Harefoot was on the throne.

> The King was so advised that he and Earl Leofric and Earl Godwin and Earl Siward, with their attendants, rode from Gloucester to Winchester unawares upon the lady (Emma of Normandy) and they bereaved her of all the treasures which she owned, which were not to be told, because before she had been very hard to the King, her son, inasmuch as she had done less for him than he would, both before he was King and after.

With Edward on the throne of England, Godwin, Earl of Wessex, began to exert a new power, using his authority over the vacillating and weak-minded ruler. Godwin's eldest son, Sweyn, was made ruler of the Welsh Marches, an important and strategic border territory; his second son, Harald, was made Earl of East Anglia; and his nephew, Beorn, was given a large estate between Northumbria and Mercia. Godwin's other sons, Tostig, Gurth, Leofwine and Wulfnoth, were too young at this time to be placed in any office; but the Earl's greatest ambition was achieved on 23 January, 1045, when his daughter, Edith, was married to Edward and became Queen of England.

It was in this atmosphere of political intrigue that Duncan's eldest son, Malcolm, was growing to manhood. The society and laws of England were totally opposed to the Celtic laws and customs of Scotland. Malcolm was brought up under the system of primogeniture, observing the theory of feudal obligation and, above all, in the belief that 'might is right'. To Malcolm, the situation in which he found himself in exile in England was a simple one. Duncan, his father, had been High King of Scotland. Therefore, as his father's eldest son, he should be High King of Scotland. MacBeth was a usurper and all it needed to depose MacBeth and place Malcolm on the Scottish throne was an army.

CHAPTER SEVEN

'MacBeth distributed money like seed'
Marianus Scotus

'Rex Scottiae Macbethad Romae argentium pauperbis seminando distribut' wrote the chronicler Marianus Scotus. 'The King of Scotland, MacBeth, distributed money like seed to the poor at Rome.' The fact that MacBeth undertook a pilgrimage to Rome in 1050 is commented on by other chroniclers, although some historians have seized upon one chronicle, the *Chronica de Mailros*, whose entry on the subject is vague, to put forward the theory that money was distributed at Rome on behalf of the Scottish king and does not necessarily mean he went to Rome in person. It seems a rather petty attempt to destroy the image of just how secure MacBeth's Scotland was compared with his neighbours' kingdoms, for the fact that MacBeth was able to leave home for a substantial period of time certainly underscores the security of his position. But Marianus Scotus, who was alive at the time of MacBeth's visit, is quite definite. MacBeth's journey to Rome is not so surprising when we learn from Irish chronicles that many Celtic rulers, from petty chieftains to High Kings, went on visits to the Holy City. It is also a matter of interest that Thorfinn Sigurdsson went on a pilgrimage to Rome about the same time.

The fact that MacBeth and Thorfinn went to Rome at the same time has caused a great deal of speculation. Some observers see in this the possibility that Thorfinn might have helped MacBeth to suppress Crinan's insurrection in 1045 and, as they had killed a prominent churchman, the pilgrimage was undertaken to seek absolution from the Pope. Others have seen MacBeth's visit as a penance for the slaying of Duncan. One nineteenth-century historian saw it as part of some evil plot to gain the Pope's favour for an invasion of England! The simple explanation is that it was a fairly normal practice for rulers with settled kingdoms to make such pilgrimages.

The *Orkneyinga Saga*, which is not to be trusted on dates, says that Thorfinn was in Rome in 1048. Other sources claim that it was Pope Leo IX who received him, which would not have been possible in 1048. Leo IX was not installed until 12 February, 1049. Thorfinn's visit probably took place during the summer of 1049. I can find no evidence to support the idea that Thorfinn was in Rome with MacBeth in 1050, although the idea is an attractive one. We are told that on his journey to Rome Thorfinn visited Harald Hardrada, Sweyn of Denmark and the German Emperor Heinrich III. According to the *Orkneyinga Saga*:

> The jarl then gave out that he meant to go south to Rome. Now when he came to Germany, he met there the Emperor Heinrich, who welcomed the jarl most cordially and gave him many magnificent gifts. He got from him a large number of horses. The jarl then rode on his journey south. He arrived at Rome and there visited the Pope and got absolution for all his sins.

It seems that this visit to Rome had a great effect on Thorfinn for, says the *Saga*, on his return to the Orkneys,

> The jarl settled down quickly and kept peace throughout his realm. He now gave up warring cruises and turned his mind to the government of his land and people, and to the making of laws. He lived usually in Birsay and had Christ's Church built there, a magnificent church. The Episcopal Seat in the Orkneys was first established there.

This is confirmed by the German chronicler Adam of Bremen (d.c. 1075) in his *Gesta Hammaburgensis Ecclesiae Pontificum*, written in the second half of the eleventh century and providing a history of the Bremen archbishopric in Norway. From the time of Olaf the diocese of Bremen had extended over a wide area, as far north as Iceland and the Norse settlements in Greenland and Vinland, the wooded land discovered by Leif Eriksson in the year

1000. It was probably part of the North American coast. Iceland and Greenland did not become independent bishoprics until the early twelfth century but, with Thorfinn's new interest in Christianity, the Orkneys were constituted an independent diocese in 1050. Adam records that 'they (the Orkneymen) had been ruled over by Irish bishops (but) our primate Adalberth, by command of the Pope, consecrated Thorulf Bishop of Birsay to take charge of them all.' Adalberth, the Archbishop of Bremen, was a native of Iceland and perhaps the first Icelander to become a bishop as the island had only been converted to Christianity fifty years before.

It was probably during the period of the Easter Synod of 1050 that the High King of Scotland arrived in Rome and, like every other prominent pilgrim, distributed money to the poor of the city. He would then have been received by Pope Leo IX. It is also likely that MacBeth and the Pope discussed the political situation in the British Isles and surrounding kingdoms. Perhaps MacBeth was called upon to justify the support of the Celtic countries for their individualist form of Christianity and asked to explain the reasoning behind these Celtic traditions. It would be odd if the subject had not come up during MacBeth's audience with the Pope, especially after the prominence given to the subject at the Easter Synod, at which Pope Leo had excommunicated the bishops of Brittany for their adherence to the ways of the Celtic Church and for refusing to submit to the archiepiscopal jurisdiction of the French city of Tours.

Pope Leo had sent a letter to Leofric, Bishop of Exeter, at about this time, praising him for having succeeded in forcing the Celtic Church in Cornwall to conform to Roman custom. By this time Cornwall had been incorporated into the English state. Athelstan (King of Wessex 925–939) finally subdued the Cornish in 936 and called himself 'King of the English and ruler of this British province'. And, although throughout the rest of the Middle Ages the official expression was *in Anglia et Cornubia*, Cornish independence and its Celtic Church were things of the past. The last primate of Cornwall died in 1040 when the diocese was combined with Devon, first at Crediton and then, in 1050, at Exeter. During this period the English reorganized the Celtic Church, disbanding the Celtic form of monasticism and converting the Celtic monastery at St Michael's Mount into a Benedictine house. Collegiate colleges such as St Buryan and Glasney were reconstituted, the parish system was introduced and, by 1050, the Celtic way of life was in a slow decline. Even so it was not until the late eighteenth century that Cornish ceased to be a spoken language.

Naturally Pope Leo was pleased to receive a report on the romanization of the Celtic Church in this province and would no doubt have discussed it with MacBeth.

Unfortunately we can find out little else about MacBeth's pilgrimage, but we cannot leave it without mentioning a story recounted by St Peter Damian which the historian H. K. Mann thought had its foundation in MacBeth's visit. St Peter Damian credits the story to Bonzio, rector of a monastery which stood near St Severeus on the Via Merulana. The story concerned a Scottish prince who, having succeeded to the throne, became disgusted by the world, its pettiness and jealousies; so he left his wife and kingdom and went on a pilgrimage to Rome. In Rome he evaded his retinue and entered Bonzio's monastery to become a monk and died there not long afterwards. The story obviously cannot concern MacBeth. Bonzio and St Peter Damian have confused H. K. Mann by the use of the word *Scotus* which, at this period, was more likely to refer to an Irishman than a Scotsman. Marianus Scotus, John Duns Scotus, Johannes (Eriugena) Scotus, Sedlius Scotus – all churchmen and scholars – were all Irishmen. But if the prince was an Irishman, might not the story have some truth? In 1064, fourteen years after MacBeth's visit, Donnchad, the son of Brian Boru, arrived in Rome on a pilgrimage. Donnchad had been King of Munster since the death of his father at Clontarf in 1014 and in 1023 became High King of Ireland. It is recorded that he died during a pilgrimage to Rome. So Bonzio's tale might possibly refer to him.

By September, 1050, MacBeth was probably on his way back to Scotland and so missed the infighting between the English and Norman bishops which took place at a special hearing in Vercelli that September. The problem had started when Edward the Confessor, who had been raised in Normandy and spoke only Norman-French, began to surround himself with Norman favourites. Robert Champart, who had been Abbot of Jumieges and had known Edward during his early years, was made Bishop of London. He had enormous influence over the King and through him a great many Norman churchmen were appointed to top positions in the English Church.

These appointments created great resentment among the English and many charges, ecclesiastical and civil, were levelled against the Normans by the English clergy and nobles. In 1050 the Norman bishop Ulf, appointed by Edward as his personal chaplain and also as Bishop of Dorchester, was forced to go to Rome to answer charges of ecclesiastical misconduct brought against him by Bishop Hereman of Sherbourne and Bishop Aldred of Worcester.

The basic reason behind this squabbling was the question of succession. Harald Hardrada of Norway and Sweyn of Denmark both claimed the English throne. Sweyn was the more active and in 1048 he sent 25 warships to raid the south coast of England. The following year he made an alliance with Gruffydd ap Llewelyn ap Seisyll, King of Gwynnedd and overlord of Wales, and a combined force of Welsh and Danes marched on England. Edward refused to move against the invaders and it was left to Aldred, Bishop of Worcester, to raise an army. The Welsh and Danes attacked and destroyed it but, for some obscure reason, retired.

Godwin was continuing to work towards the fulfilment of his ambition by placing his family in key positions in the kingdom, but he now began to find himself thwarted by Edward who favoured the Normans. And it was the coming of the Normans which had such a disastrous effect on Celtic Scotland.

Norman churchmen, such as Bishop Ulf, whose position was endorsed by the Roman cardinals in spite of the hearing that September, seemed to be preparing the way for a Norman take-over of England and the succession of William, Duke of Normandy. William was born in 1028, the son of Robert, Count of Hiesmois, and his mistress Herleva (or Arletta), daughter of Fulbert, a tanner of Falaise. There could be no marriage between Robert and his mistress, so William was illegitimate. Robert, shortly afterwards, became Duke of Normandy but died in 1035, and the seven-year-old William succeeded. On coming of age he soon proved that he was well equipped to rule.

In late 1042 he had, like so many others, turned his eyes to the throne of England. Undaunted by the claims of Harald Hardrada, Sweyn of Denmark, the ambitious Earl Godwin and another Edward Aetheling in exile in Hungary, William decided to establish a claim himself and, in 1050, married Matilda, daughter of Baldwin V of Flanders, who claimed descent from King Alfred. Under the laws of primogeniture he was thus provided with a tenuous link to the throne. His stronger advantage was his influence over Edward the Confessor, whose sympathies, as we have seen, were far closer to Normandy than to England. In 1051 William visited Edward at Westminster and it is thought that he secured a promise there that he would be named as his successor.

William realized that his greatest rival was Earl Godwin and through his agents, the Norman churchmen, he made moves to eliminate him. The first trial of strength came when the primacy of England became vacant in 1050. Edward, prompted by the Norman bishops, wanted to make Robert Champert, then Bishop of London, Archbishop of Canterbury. The chapter of the province met hurriedly in the cathedral and, in spite of Edward's wishes, elected Aelfric, a relation of Godwin, to the archbishopric. The struggle between the opposing factions continued until mid-Lent.

The nobles who surrounded Edward and who constituted the Witenagemot had often come into conflict with Earl Godwin during his forceful and bloody climb to become the premier lord of England. They therefore rejoiced at Godwin's fall from favour with Edward and their hatred of him was stronger than their hatred of the Normans. The Witenagemot met in London in mid-Lent, 1051, and declared that Robert Champert should be appointed Archbishop and Aelfric's election declared null-and-void.

At this time Count Eustace of Boulogne arrived in England to visit Edward and, on his return journey, there was rioting as he passed through Dover. The English maintained that the count and his men had started the affair by riding into the town in full armour and demanding food and quarters as if they were conquerors. In the rioting that followed several people were killed. As Dover was governed by Earl Godwin, Edward summoned him and demanded that he punish the town with the utmost severity for insulting Count Eustace. Godwin refused. Archbishop Champert now moved in for the *coup de grace*. He resurrected the charge against Godwin of the murder of Edward's brother, Alfred Aetheling. Edward summoned Godwin to appear before the Witenagemot at Gloucester to answer the charge. Godwin refused and the country sprang to arms as the prospect of a civil war loomed.

Siward of Northumbria and Leofric of Mercia prepared to march against Godwin but, at the last moment, hostilities were averted by a proposal that the Witenagemot adjourn to meet in London at Michaelmas. Robert Champert had, meanwhile, placed sufficient bribes with members of the Witenagemot to secure a conviction against Godwin.

Learning this, Godwin again refused to appear and Edward pronounced a sentence of exile against every member of the Godwin family. They were all ordered to leave the country within five days and condemned to forfeit all their possessions. Even Edward's wife, Edith, was sent as a prisoner to a convent at Wherwell, Hampshire, where his half-sister was the abbess.

By early October, 1051, Godwin, his wife, and three of his sons – Sweyn, Tostig and Gurth – were in Flanders sheltering with Baldwin V. His other sons, Harold and Leofwine, managed to escape from the West Country, embarking at Avonmouth. They sought shelter at the court of Diarmaid Mac Mael na mBó, the King of Leinster.

The Norman favourites of King Edward were now left in control in England and even Leofric of Mercia and Siward of Northumbria became concerned as Normans were appointed to all positions of authority in the country. The Godwins, however, had not given up entirely. During the months in exile, Godwin in Flanders and Harold in Ireland prepared to invade England. Their chief agent in England was Stigand, Bishop of Winchester, who had been a supporter of Emma of Normandy. Now Stigand secretly pledged his allegiance to Godwin.

Towards the end of June, Earl Godwin left Flanders for England with a large fleet and his son Harold left Ireland with a smaller fleet of nine ships. The Normans, acting in Edward's name, gathered a fleet at Sandwich but did not seem willing to give battle. Unopposed, Godwin sailed along the south coast to the Isle of Wight, attacking and harrying coastal towns. Harold, meanwhile, landed at Porlock where he won a decisive victory before returning to his ships, sailing around the Cornish coast and joining his father's fleet.

The English, realizing that it was a choice between Godwin and the Normans, rose up in Godwin's support. By September, 1052, Godwin had sailed up the Thames to London and returned to his mansion in Southwark. No opposition was offered while his army mustered on the south bank opposite the city. The Normans were panic-stricken. Robert Champert, the Archbishop of Canterbury, and Bishop Ulf of Dorchester were among the first to make a dash to safety, reaching the coast near Naze in Essex where they managed to board a ship for Normandy.

Godwin summoned the Witenagemot and formally refuted all charges made against him. The weak-minded Edward then formally declared a full restitution of all the Godwin estates and offices. Queen Edith was recalled to court from her convent prison and tokens of royal favour were showered on the Godwins. Godwin himself did not live long enough to enjoy his success. He was struck down by an illness on 14 September, 1052, and died at Winchester in 1053 while he and his sons, Harold and Tostig, were spending Easter with the King.

These events in England had a direct effect on Scotland. When, in September, 1052, the Normans fled from England, several of them travelled northwards and crossed the border into Scotland. Florence of Worcester records that MacBeth gave shelter to many Norman fugitives and incurred the wrath of powerful English nobles. It is highly unlikely that there was any political motive behind MacBeth's act of hospitality. We must remember that he was closely bound by Celtic law and custom, and the laws of hospitality are very clearly defined and constitute a code of honour. Travellers were always afforded a generous welcome. Each clan had to have, by law, a public hostel which was looked after by a full-time manager who had to maintain the roads leading to it and to keep a light burning all night to aid travellers. Such hostels were maintained from the poorest clan to the royal hostel at Scone.

The code of hospitality was so strong that, even if there was not firm evidence to the contrary, it could be said with some assurance that it would have been impossible for Duncan to be killed in the way Shakespeare specifies, for such a violation of a sacred Celtic law was unthinkable and MacBeth would never have killed Duncan while he was a guest under his own roof. The code of hospitality is frequently underlined in Celtic mythology: perhaps the most famous instance is the story of the Court of Dá Derga in the Ulster Cycle.

MacBeth, in giving hospitality to the Norman fugitives from England, was therefore not expressing a preference but simply carrying out the dictates of his social code. But by so doing MacBeth seems to have given the young Malcolm Mac Duncan means by which to advance his own ambitious plans.

Malcolm was now twenty-one years old and had been in exile in England for twelve years. It is from about this time that the court in England seems to have taken his claims to the kingship of Scotland seriously. Plans for an invasion of Scotland, the purpose of which was to place young Malcolm on the throne, with Malcolm then acknowledging the suzerainty of Edward the Confessor, were considered for the first time.

CHAPTER EIGHT

'Earl Siward went with a large army into Scotland'
Anglo-Saxon Chronicle

By the early summer of 1054, Malcolm Mac Duncan had argued his case so successfully at the English court that he was able to obtain support for his plan to invade Scotland and overthrow MacBeth. Some of the English chroniclers, notably Florence of Worcester, maintained that Malcolm had King Edward's personal support and that Edward had delegated command of the invasion forces to Siward, Earl of Northumbria.

Siward was one of the Danes who had risen to power in England with the Danish dynasty and had carved out a small empire for himself as one of the three premier earls in the country. He had married Elfleda, daughter of Ealdred of Northumbria, and had become earl on the death of Ealdred, claiming the inheritance through his wife. His cousin was Malcolm's mother and this family connection was, perhaps, another reason for his support of the exiled Scot. But the ambitious earl must also have seen new territories to be won in Scotland for his own personal wealth and glorification.

According to some chroniclers he was called Siward Dirga, or Siward the Stout, or Valiant. But their account of his career is so remarkably similar to that of Sigurd Hlodversson, the father of Thorfinn, who was also called the Stout, that it seems probable that the careers of these Norse jarls have become confused. Siward, we are told, enjoyed a restless youth adventuring in the Orkneys, where he slew a dragon. He met the Norse god Odin who foretold his greatness and gave him a wonderous banner, 'the land-frightening raven'. More accurately, we are told that he became a favourite of Edward of England after he had cut down the rebellious Jarl Tosti on a little bridge near London and had dropped his head at Edward's feet.

Professor Stevens, in *Macbeth, Earl Siward and Dundee* (1876), says:

> Jarl Siward called Dirga, the Stout or Valiant, was one of those noble stalwart figures which will never pass away from the pages of tradition. Truth and fiction in his story cannot now be narrowly scanned, but we know enough of his career to call him in iron strength, piercing wit and wisdom, loftiness of character and indomitable defiance of danger and death … the last of the jarls.

This was the man who was to plan and conduct the campaign against the High King of Scotland. With young Malcolm accompanying him, Siward began to move his army into Scotland in July, 1054. He had gathered a large force of Northumbrians, comprising Anglo-Saxons and Danes. The *Anglo-Saxon Chronicle* states:

> Earl Siward went with a large army into Scotland, both with a naval force and a land force, and fought against the Scots, of whom he made a great slaughter and put them to flight, and the King escaped. Many also fell on his own side, both Danish and English, and also his own son Oshern, and his sister's son, Siward, and some of his 'huscurls' and also of the king's were there slain, on the day of the seven sleepers, that is July 27.

It seems that Siward's objective was to take the Scottish capital at Scone. As his army marched north it appears to have encountered surprisingly little resistance. This could have been part of MacBeth's strategy, to allow the invading forces to march well inside his territory before confronting them. It could also be that MacBeth was unsure of the loyalty of the Atholl clansmen and he did not want to fight a battle which placed the Atholl territory at his back between himself and his own clan lands of Moray. So Siward's army was able to cross the Forth by way of Stirling and march towards Perth itself, crossing the Tay on its way to Scone. In the meantime Siward's fleet had sailed into the Firth of Tay, providing the Earl not only with supplies and reinforcements, but acting as a protection for one flank of his army.

The battle between MacBeth's forces and the invaders which took place on 27 July, 1054, has been immortalized by Shakespeare as the day when 'Birnam Wood do come to Dunsinane'. Certainly Dunsinnan, which lies close by Scone between Perth and Dundee, is a likely spot for the battle. Contemporary sources merely state that the site was in the vicinity of the Scottish capital and they dispel the Shakespearian notion that MacBeth and the Scottish army were cowering behind the walls of some fortress, for the Scots met the Northumbrians in a fierce, open conflict. But it is possible to be more specific as to the location of the battle site.

Professor George Stevens is of the opinion that the site was close by Dundee. He dismisses the popular theory that the town of Dundee was founded by Earl David in 1160 who piously called it *Donum Dei*, the Gift of God. Indeed Dundee is merely an anglicization of the Gaelic name Dùn Dèagh, the fortress of Deagh. Certainly there was a settlement near the modern site long before 1160 and there is a fortress four miles from the town which the nineteenth-century archaeologist Dr Joseph Robertson described as 'the Dundee of the 9th Century'.

Professor Stevens insists that the battle site was actually at Dundee. The earliest chronicler to name Dundee as the site was William of Malmesbury, writing early in the twelfth century, who says: 'But the Earl (Siward) listening to his (Malcolm) prayer, collected his army and marched in aid of the King as far as Dundee'.

But Stevens presents his own evidence in support of his claim. In the late nineteenth century he found a runic memorial stone at Högby, East Gotland, in Sweden, which dated from the mid-eleventh century. The inscription has been translated as follows:

> Thukir raised this stone in memory of Asur Sen, his uncle; death grasped that gallant one out east in Greece.
>
> Five belted sons were born to Guli. Fell on Fur Isle fearless Armundi. Neath Greek skies, out east, lies Asur Grim-Axe. Bathing in Bornholm bled my Halfdan. At Dundee sank Kari and Buri is also dead.
>
> These runes were carved by Thukir.

Professor Stevens emphasizes the importance of the fact that Kari, the fourth son of Guli, fell, presumably in battle, at Dundee. A battle at Dundee, coupled with the fact that the stone dates from the mid-eleventh century is, he feels, too much of a coincidence, remembering that Siward's army was full of Danes. He writes: 'I therefore unhesitatingly claim this block as apparently another proof of authentic history, a granite argument in proof of the main facts connected with MacBeth.'

The *Annals of Ulster* says that 3,000 Scots were killed in the battle while 1,500 English and Danes were slain. As the Irish historians of this period would have no cause to play down English losses, we can certainly assume that far more Scots than English and Danes died. But was the battle the complete victory the English chroniclers record? In spite of the casualties suffered by the Scots, it would appear that the battle was drawn. The *Anglo Saxon Chronicle*, while awarding victory to Siward, admits that his army suffered heavy casualties, especially among its leaders, and this is borne out by the fact that Siward had to withdraw his invasion force from Scotland without fulfilling his primary objective – the overthrow of MacBeth and the establishment of Malcolm as king.

Siward undoubtedly suffered some important casualties. Perhaps the casualty which caused him the most pain was the death of his son Oshern. According to later tradition, Siward, on hearing that his son had been killed, asked whether he had been wounded in the chest or in the back. In other words, had he been wounded facing his enemies or fleeing from them? On learning that his son had been wounded in the chest he commented: 'I can then be glad for so was he worthy of me and himself.'

In the battle scene (Act V, Scene 8) of his play, Shakespeare uses this story to good effect:

Ross. Your son, my lord, has paid a soldier's debt:
  He only lived but till he was a man;
  The which no sooner had his prowess confirmed
  In the unshrinking station where he fought,
  But, like a man, he died.
Siward.   Then he is dead?
Ross. Ay, and brought off the field: your cause of sorrow
  Must not be measured by his worth, for then

86

It hath not end.
Siward.   Had he his hurts before?
Ross. Ay, on the front.
Siward.   Why then, God's soldier be he.
   Had I as many sons as I have hairs
   I would not wish them to a fairer death.
   And so his knell is knolled.
Malcolm.   He's worth more sorrow,
   And that I'll spend for him.
Siward.   He's worth no more:
   They say he parted well, and paid his score.
   And so, God be with him.

Another important casualty on Siward's side was his nephew, Siward. The *Annals of Ulster* also claim that one Dorfinn, the son of Finntuir, was killed. Later historians claim that Dorfinn was the son of Thorfinn Sigurdsson because it was by the name Finntuir that the Irish knew him. But, apart from it being improbable that a son of Thorfinn would be found fighting against MacBeth, Thorfinn and his wife, Ingibjorg, only had two sons, Paul and Erlend. The mystery of Dorfinn, who must have been of some importance for the chroniclers to note his name, remains unsolved. One theory put forward is that the chronicler mistook his patrynomic and this Dorfinn was, in reality, Dolfinn, son of Malcolm's cousin, Gospadruig, who was now styling himself King of Cumbria.

Several legends sprang up about this battle. The most popular was the prophecy of the three weird sisters that MacBeth would not be defeated until 'Birnam Wood do come to Dunsinane'. This prophecy was supposedly fulfilled when Malcolm ordered his soldiers to cut branches from the trees in Birnam Wood to use as camouflage when they advanced on MacBeth's stronghold at Dunsinane. According to Shakespeare, echoing this legend, (Act V, Scene 4):

Siward. What wood is this before us?
Menteith.   The wood of Birnam.
Malcolm. Let every soldier hew him down a bough
   And bear't before him, thereby shall we shadow
   The numbers of our host and make discovery
   Err in report of us.

It is a nice piece of drama but one with no substantiation in fact.

The Menzies clan still believe in that legend and that Crinan, the Mormaer of Atholl, was the chief of their clan. They further believe that when Malcolm invaded Scotland, the entire clan turned out for him and that they were chosen to lead the advance on Dunsinane bearing branches of rowan or mountain ash. So firmly do the clan Menzies believe in this legend that the clan badge is a sprig of rowan or mountain ash and their hunting tartan, a nineteenth-century invention like most tartans, also repeats the colours of the rowan tree – green for the leaves and scarlet for the berries. However, the first Menzies was a Norman knight named de Menyers who settled in Dumfries. The name was subsequently turned into Menzies and is always pronounced *Mengies*, although the spelling is with a 'z'. This has always puzzled those not brought up in Scotland. The Gaelic letter for 'g' ȝ can be mistaken by the unwary for a 'z' and was probably copied in error and has since become the standard spelling.

Perhaps the most important point reflecting on Siward's battle with MacBeth is that the *Anglo-Saxon Chronicle* makes no mention of Malcolm, merely recording that Siward invaded Scotland, was victorious in battle and 'carried off a large amount of plunder such as had never been captured before'. But the English accounts are somewhat confused and contradictory. The *Chronica de Mailros* claims that Siward put MacBeth to flight and placed Malcolm on the throne of Scotland. Another chronicler, Langtoft, says that MacBeth was made a prisoner and that the kingdom was given to 'Malcolm of Cumberland'. Yet another chronicler, Gaimor, says that Earl Siward made an agreement with the High King of Scotland following his victory, 'but MacBeth destroyed the peace and ceased not to carry on the war'. A communication from the court of Edward the Confessor to Pope Boniface says: 'Edward, the King of England, gave the kingdom of Scotland to be held of him to Malcolm, the son of the King of the Cumbrians'.

Florence of Worcester, who incidentally refers to the fact that the Normans who sought shelter with MacBeth in 1052 were killed in the battle, states that Siward was only able to establish Malcolm as King of Cumbria and that this was done by the order of Edward the Confessor. Most of the other contemporary chroniclers agree that, in spite of the claims of his cousin Gospadruig Mac Maldred to his petty kingship, Malcolm was recognized as King of Cumbria from this time onwards. Cumbria was obviously the only part of the Scottish kingdom over which the Northumbrians had gained any control.

It is of note that Marianus Scotus calls Malcolm *'filius regis Cumbrorum'*, the son of the King of Cumbria and not of Scotland. The letter from the English court to Pope Boniface also says that Malcolm was 'son of the King of Cumbrians'. It is quite true that Duncan was made King of Cumbria under his grandfather, Malcolm II, but when he was installed as High King in 1035 the office had gone to his brother Maldred. In recognizing Duncan only as King of Cumbria and not High King of Scotland, the chroniclers seem to imply that Duncan was not recognized as the legitimate heir of Malcolm II. Even Symeon of Durham regards MacBeth as the *heir* to Malcolm II and not the successor to Duncan I.

To sum up Siward's campaign of 1054, a partial success was achieved by establishing Malcolm as the king of the most southerly Scottish province of Cumbria. Although the High King of Scotland's army suffered nearly twice as many casualties as Siward's army at Dundee, MacBeth's men succeeded in inflicting enough casualties on the invading army to turn it back. Any further plans for a conquest of Scotland by Siward were cut short by his death the following year.

Siward died at York after a short illness. While on his deathbed he told his followers: 'I will not die like a cow!' He asked to be dressed in full armour and, grasping his shield and battle-axe, was lifted up to die on his feet. It was reminiscent of the pagan Viking funerals, but then Siward was a Danish jarl. The chroniclers recorded: 'And he lies at Galmachó in the monastery that he himself had caused to be built and to be consecrated in the name of God and Olaf.' A church to St Olaf exists in the parish of St Olave Mary-Gate to the north-west of York City. And 'Siward's How' is the name of a small hill to the south-east.

Malcolm had now lost his strongest supporter. Waltheof, Siward's second son and heir, was still a child. The Godwin family, now in firm political control of England, persuaded

Edward to give the earldom to Tostig, one of the Godwin brothers. Tostig Godwinson was the third son of the dead Earl of Wessex and was regarded by Edward as his favourite brother-in-law. Tostig seemed to enjoy an ascendancy over the pliable king and already jealousy was building up between him and his older brother, Harold. Tostig also appears to have been very friendly with Malcolm; they probably grew up at the English court together. As the new Earl of Northumbria, Tostig took up Malcolm's cause with renewed vigour and gave full support to the young man's plans for further invasions of Scotland.

CHAPTER NINE

'On the floor of Scone he will vomit blood'

St Berchan

Three years after Siward's unsuccessful attempt to place Malcolm on the throne of Scotland MacBeth was slain by Malcolm at Lumphanan in Mar on 15 August, 1057. MacBeth was fifty-two years old and had ruled the country for seventeen years.

We must surmise that during the three years between 1054 and 1057 Scotland was under continual attack from the south. The fact that Malcolm, even with a strong English army, took three years to overthrow MacBeth is indicative of the allegiance of the Scottish people to their High King. But we must concede that Malcolm, having established his base as King of Cumbria, probably started to subvert the Cumbrian Celts to his cause, and eventually some of the Atholl clans, who would have been induced to support Malcolm out of clan loyalty. However, there is no indication as to who was Mormaer of Atholl immediately after the death of Crinan in 1045 and whether he supported MacBeth or not. What is clear is that early in 1057 MacBeth was still in control of the Scottish capital and that the major part of the country was still loyal to him.

During these three years in which the Scots were fighting English incursions, there is no mention of them receiving aid from Thorfinn Sigurdsson nor any other help from neighbouring countries. If MacBeth had any influence with the Vatican, arising from his visit to Rome, such contact ended with the death of Pope Leo IX in April, 1054. Leo IX died a prisoner in the Vatican, having led an unsuccessful Papal army, consisting mainly of Germans, against the Normans in the south of Italy. The same year, according to Tighernach, the bishop who had installed MacBeth as High King, Maelduin Mac Gille-Odrain, Bishop of St Andrews and Primate of Scotland, also died. According to contemporary chroniclers, Bishop Maelduin was well respected outside Scotland and might have been able to use his influence to bring pressure on England to desist from attacks on Scotland. He was replaced as primate by Bishop Tuthald.

In trying to reconstruct the sequence of events leading to MacBeth's death, the Hon. Stuart Erskine, in *Macbeth: being an historical figure*, turns to a passage in St Berchan's writings which he maintains is significant. This passage has previously been translated as:

> In the middle of Scone it will vomit blood
> The evening of a night in much contention.

Erskine, however, believes the passage has been misinterpreted. It had been thought that this is St Berchan's reference to the battle between MacBeth and Siward in 1054. Erskine thinks that the passage applies to the year 1057 and that the translation carries the wrong emphasis. The line *For lar Scoine sceithfidh full* he renders into modern Gaelic as *Air lar Sgàin sgeithidh é fuil* which he translates as 'On the floor of Scone he (MacBeth) will vomit blood'. Erskine contends, perhaps tenuously, that MacBeth was surprised by Malcolm's men in the *bruigheann* (royal residence) at Scone. He claims that MacBeth was attacked and wounded but managed to escape. Therefore he bled on the floor of the palace of Scone as Berchan indicates. But he did not die there.

It is a fascinating piece of reconstruction but I doubt whether it would have been possible for a band of Malcolm's men to enter the royal residence, surprise the court and get near enough to the High King to launch a murderous attack on him without warning. Even in the seventh century, according to one of the earliest Irish texts of the tale *The Court of Dá Derg*, the retinue of a High King was quite extensive when in residence at his court. At that time the High King was described as being surrounded by nine pipers, nine harpers, his chief minstrel, three poets, three entertainers (such as jugglers), three chief judges, equerries, cupbearers, two private attendants, charioteers, outriders, nine guardsmen – warriors of high reputation who always accompanied the High King – and the High King's principal hostages. It would therefore have been difficult to ambush MacBeth in his own palace.

What is certain is that MacBeth set out from Scone and made for the northern clan lands of Moray, presumably in an attempt to reach his own clansmen and perhaps raise them against Malcolm. He would have left Scone heading first towards Brechin and then perhaps along Glen Esk, by the North Esk River, before crossing the hills into Mar. Perhaps he was trying to reach the immediate shelter of the monastic settlement at Aboyne before crossing the Grampian Mountains into his own clan territory. Pressing quite closely on his heels, so it seems, was a body of Malcolm's men.

MacBeth and his bodyguard would have passed the River Dee at a ford near Craig Ferrar (Creag Faire – the Rock of Watching) and, while skirting the base of this height, tradition has it that he was attacked by Malcolm's troops near to the town of Tarland. It is said that his bodyguard was attacked on Queen's Hill, a thickly wooded spur of the hill of Mortlich, which rises to a height of 1,248 feet and dominates the area of Cromar. Situated on the eastern side of the hill is 'MacBeth's Well' where tradition has it that the High King refreshed himself on his northward flight. Just to the north-east of Mortlich is the town of Lumphanan.

MacBeth, probably driven to Lumphanan by the skirmish with Malcolm's men, found himself cut off from the safety of Aboyne and decided to make a stand here. By the roadside at Lumphanan there is a stone circle called Peel Ring. Tradition has it that this was where MacBeth fell in battle, leading a charge of his bodyguard against Malcolm's troops. The contemporary chroniclers simply say that MacBeth, the High King of Scotland, was slain by Malcolm, *King of Cumbria*. The *Chronica de Mailros* records: 'Duncan's son, named Malcolm, cut off his (Macbeth) reign by *a cruel death* in Lumphanan'.

This is not the record of an evil tyrant's, or usurper's, death by a righteous and virtuous prince, as Shakespeare would have us believe. MacBeth's body was taken to the holy island of Iona and buried there with all the pomp and ceremony accorded to a lawful High King of Scotland. The record of his burial at Iona emphasizes the fact that MacBeth was in no way considered a usurper by the people of Scotland, as no unlawful king was allowed to be buried there. Furthermore, when Malcolm's body was brought back to Scotland for burial he was interred at Dunfermline, thus becoming, significantly I believe, the first Scottish King to be denied the traditional burial on the holy island.

Even those historians who, 350 years later, began to lay the foundations for the myth of the evil, tyrannical Macbeth of Shakespeare's vision, echo contemporary chroniclers in their praise of MacBeth as a ruler.

According to Andrew Wyntoun in his *Orygynale Cronykil of Scotland*:

> And sevyntene wyntyr full rygnand
> As king he wes than in till Scotland
> All hys tyme wes gret plente
> Abowndand bath in land and se
> He wes in justice rycht lawchfull.
> And till hys legis all awfull.

> And seventeen winters full he reigned
> As king he was in Scotland.
> All his time was great plenty
> Abounding both on land and sea.
> He was in justice right lawful
> And to his liege men all awe-full.

And William Stewart, as late as 1531–35 in his poetical translation of Boece entitled *The Buik of the Chronicles of Scotland*, says:

> This Macbeth quhilk wes bayth wuss and wycht
> Strang in ane stour and trew as ony stull
> Defender als with of the common weill
> So just ane judge, so equal and so treww
> As be his deids richt weill befoir ay schew.

> This MacBeth was both wise and strong
> Strong in argument and true as any steel.
> Defender always of the common weal

So just a judge, so equal and so true
As by his deed right well before us show.

Stewart emphasizes:

Baith speir and scheild to all kirkmen wes he,
And merchandis alls that saillit on the se,
To husbandmen that laborit on the ground
Ane better king in no tyme micht be found.

Both spear and shield to all churchmen was he
And merchants all who sailed upon the sea,
To husbandmen who laboured on the land
No better king in any time might be found.

The picture that history presents us with – the High King of Scotland leading a last valiant charge against his assassins – is far different from Shakespeare's account.

And what of Macduff who, according to Shakespeare, slew MacBeth to revenge the wrongs the king had done him? Did he exist? What of this Scottish 'noble' born of a Caesarian birth to fulfil the witches' prophecy that no man born of woman would kill MacBeth? Is there no truth in that final scene where Macbeth, confronted by Macduff, cries:

I will not yield,
To kiss the ground before young Malcolm's feet,
And to be baited with the rabble's curse.
Though Birnam Wood do come to Dunsinane,
And thou opposed, being of no woman born,
Yet I will try the last. Before my body
I throw my war-like shield. Lay on, Macduff;
And damned be him that first cries 'Hold, enough!'

Macduff appears in none of the contemporary accounts. John of Fordun, in 1384, conjures up Macduff but merely records that he went into exile because of his friendship with Duncan's sons. Andrew Wyntoun, however, writing between about 1395 and 1428, is the first to give Macduff credit for killing MacBeth, and even Wyntoun's tale differs vastly from later chroniclers who added their own embellishments to the story which eventually led to Shakespeare's creation.

When Wyntoun introduces Macduff he makes him a Scottish

'noble' from Fife who has to flee to England because he is friendly with Malcolm and Donald Ban. Wyntoun says nothing of any attempt made by MacBeth to kill Macduff's wife or, indeed, his children. Wyntoun says that when MacBeth heard of Macduff's intended flight from the Scottish court to his estate at Kennawchy he followed him there 'and felny gret there wald have done', but Macduff's wife waylaid MacBeth and kept him occupied until her husband had escaped by boat from Earlsferry across the Firth of Forth. Nowhere does Wyntoun state that MacBeth slew Macduff's wife or children.

Hector Boece (c. 1465–1536) may be credited with many inventions to the MacBeth story and was the first Scottish historian who accused MacBeth of the slaughter of Macduff's wife and children. Boece also invented the character of Banquo, the poisoning of Duncan, the character of Lady MacBeth and the three weird sisters.

Speaking purely from an artistic viewpoint, it would have been more dramatic, surely, if Malcolm had slain Macbeth in the Shakespearian drama? In trying to copy the inventions of historians, Shakespeare was led into a rather cumbersome side plot with several contradictions. For example, why did Macduff fly and leave his wife and children in a tyrant's hands? Macduff, the fictional character, is certainly no coward as painted in his final scene with Macbeth. When he learns of the death of his wife and children, he declares:

Front to front
Bring thou this fiend of Scotland and myself,
Within my sword's length set him;

But the primary question – 'Why in that rawness left you wife and child?' – is one that he cannot answer very well. Certainly Shakespeare realized this weak point and through the character of Ross and Lady Macduff tries to frame an answer to the question (Act IV, Scene 2):

Enter Lady Macduff, her Son, and Ross.
Lady Macduff. What had he done to make him fly the land?
Ross. You must have patience, madam.
Lady Macduff.   He had none:
His flight was madness; when our actions do not,

96

Our fears do make us traitors.
Ross.   You know not
    Whether it was his wisdom or his fear.
Lady Macduff. Wisdom! To leave his wife, to leave his babes,
    His mansion and his tithes, in a place
    From whence himself does fly? He loves us not.
    He wants the natural touch; for the poor wren,
    The most diminuitive of birds, will fight,
    Her young ones in her nest, against the owl.
    All is the fear and nothing is the love,
    As little is the wisdom, where the flight
    So runs against all reason.

Shakespeare believed he was recounting history and let himself be influenced by the historians who had, in fact, conjured Macduff out of thin air. Shakespeare certainly made the best of the material available and it can be no slur on his craftmanship that Macduff is a weak point of the play.

Malcolm Mac Duncan, having slain MacBeth, was unable to press home his advantage. Scotland did not fall to him. We must assume from subsequent events that no sooner was MacBeth dead than his assassins had to retreat from Lumphanan, deep in Scottish territory, to the south again. Two facts emphasize this point. First that the body of MacBeth was taken by his followers and, with Tuthald, the new primate of Scotland, the dead ruler's cortège was allowed to go in peace to Iona where the body was buried. Secondly, and most important, there was the election of a new High King of Scotland at Scone which is simply recorded in the chronicle of *Duan Albannach*: 'After MacBeth of renown, seven months of the reign of Lulach.'

Late in August, 1057, Lulach, MacBeth's stepson, the son of his wife Gruoch and Gillecomgain, was elected by the mormaers, chieftains and churchmen of Scotland to the High Kingship and installed in the traditional way at Scone. This would indicate that Scone was still firmly in the hands of the MacBeth faction and that Malcolm was still regarded as a foreign usurper unfit to be elected to the office. Tighernach, the *Annals of Loch Cé*, Marianus Scotus and John of Fordun all agree that the twenty-five year old Lulach was properly elected and was recognized by all as 'High

King of Scotland', 'King of Scots' and 'King of Scotia'. Lulach, at this time, was married with a son and daughter and lived in the district of Lochaber.

Latin chronicles refer to him as Lulach the Fool (*Fatuus*). The name would not have arisen from a Celtic nickname, which usually referred to some physical aspect of a person, because Lulach could not have been mentally retarded. Under Celtic law no person could be elected to office if they possessed any major physical handicap. The reason why he was subsequently regarded as a fool is lost in the mists of history. It may be that he made some miscalculation during his military campaign against Malcolm and so earned the epithet.

We know that Lulach held out against Malcolm's invading Northumbrian forces, now possibly reinforced by Cumbrians and Atholl clansmen, for seven months and three days after the death of MacBeth. One chronicler records that he was slain 'by stratagem' at Essy in Strathbogie in modern-day Aberdeenshire, on 17 March, 1058. Tighernach records that on this date 'Lulach, High King of Scotland, was treacherously slain by Malcolm Mac Duncan'. The recording of the fact that he was slain 'by stratagem' and 'treacherously' would indicate that Lulach did not die in open battle with Malcolm's forces but that he died at the hands of Malcolm's agents. Again it is significant to note that Lulach, too, was buried at Iona.

On 25 April, 1058, the twenty-seven-year-old Malcolm, after three years of vicious warfare in which he had slain two legally elected High Kings of Scotland, was crowned by Bishop Tuthald at Scone.

Lulach's children were still in their infancy and not eligible for election to office. They appear to have been smuggled out of Scone to Moray for their upbringing. This is confirmed by the fact that, on reaching his majority, Mael Snechta or Malsnectai (Snow's Servant), the son of Lulach, became Mormaer of Moray. Malsnectai is recorded as granting certain lands to the culdees of the Abbey of Deer near Aberdeen. Malcolm III regarded Malsnectai with deep suspicion and hatred, seeing in him a rival claimant for the throne. After nursing this suspicion and hatred for twenty years, Malcolm, in 1078, managed to expel Malsnectai from Scotland. According to the *Book of Deer*, the *Annals of*

Ulster and the *Orderic Vitalis,* Malsnectai 'ended his life unhappily' as a monk in 1085.

That was not the end of the House of Moray, for Lulach's daughter had a son named Angus who, on the banishment of Malsnectai, was elected Mormaer of Moray in his place. He was slain with 4,000 Moray clansmen at a battle at Strathathro, in Forfar, in 1130. After this the Moray claim to the High Kingship appears to have died out. The claim of Moray had been made under the old Celtic Law system and by the mid-twelfth century this system was being displaced throughout Scotland. Norman law, the law of primogeniture, was certainly in force among the new nobility, the landowners and the Scottish court.

MacBeth's powerful cousin, Thorfinn Sigurdsson, the Jarl of the Orkneys, who had been responsible for placing him on the throne, did not, as we have seen, come to Scotland's aid during the struggles against Malcolm and the English. The reason appears to be that Thorfinn was dead. Some chroniclers have significantly placed the date of his death as 1057, the same year as MacBeth's. There is no evidence for this, although we can be certain that Thorfinn was dead before 1059, because it was in that year that Malcolm, now Malcolm III, married Ingibjorg, Thorfinn's widow, who then bore Malcolm three sons, Duncan II, Malcolm and Donald.

As previously pointed out, the dates from the *Orkneyinga Saga* are confusing and inaccurate. The *Saga* says that from 1014 Thorfinn ruled the Orkneys for seventy winters. *St Olaf's Saga* cuts this down to sixty. Yet both contradict themselves and say he died in the latter days of the reign of Harald Hardrada who was killed at the Battle of Stamford Bridge, Yorkshire, in 1066. But Malcolm's eldest son, Duncan, was born in 1059. Some historians have tried to correct these discrepancies by suggesting that the ancient chroniclers made a mistake and that the Ingibjorg Malcolm married was Thorfinn's daughter and not his widow. However, we know that Thorfinn had only two children – both sons. These sons, Paul and Erlend, later ruled the Orkney jarldom between them.

Whether Thorfinn died in 1057 or not, it is obvious from the accounts that he did not meet his death in battle. Therefore the significance given to this by some historians – indicating that

Thorfinn died fighting with MacBeth — is misplaced. The *Heimskringla* states that 'he died of disease'. My belief is that he died of some illness before he was able to go to the aid of MacBeth. His death could have taken place as early as 1054.

All the Norse writers lament the passing of the greatest jarl ever seen in the Orkneys. According to the *Orkneyinga Saga*:

> Jarl Thorfinn held all his dominions till his death day. It is truly said that he has been the most powerful of all jarls of the Orkneymen; he possessed nine jarldoms in Scotland, and all the Hebrides, and a great dominion in Ireland. So says Arnor, the jarl's poet:
> 'To the ring hater was subject a host (I tell the people the truth how Thorfinn was esteemed) from Thursa-sker to Dublin'.
> Jarl Thorfinn was five winters old when Malcolm, King of Scots, his mother's father, gave him the name of jarl, and he was jarl after that for seventy winters. He died in the latter days of Harald, Sigurd's son.

The *Heimskringla of St Olaf's Saga* echoes closely this passage:

> Jarl Thorfinn, Sigurd's son, has been the noblest jarl in the islands, and has had great dominions, of all the jarls of the Orkneymen. He possessed Shetlands and Orkneys (and) the Hebrides, he also had a great dominion in Scotland and Ireland. Of this Arnor, the jarl's poet, said:
> 'To the ring hater was subject a host (I tell the people truth how Thorfinn was esteemed) from Thursa-sker to Dublin'.
> Thorfinn was the greatest warrior. He took the jarldom when he was five winters old and he ruled for more than sixty winters; and he died of disease in the latter days of Harald Sigurd's son. But Brusi died in the days of Canute the Powerful a little after the fall of King Olaf the Holy.

Flatey's Book of St Olaf's Saga records with a surprising degree of honesty for the time:

> Thorfinn is buried at Christ's Church in Birsay, which he had caused to be built. The jarl was much lamented in this inherited lands; but in those lands that he laid under him with warfare, many men thought it great servitude to live under his dominion. Then many of the dominions that the jarl had laid under himself were lost; and men sought for themselves the protection of chieftains that were native born to the dominions. Loss followed quickly upon the decease of the Jarl Thorfinn.

Certainly, had it not been for Thorfinn Sigurdsson, MacBeth might not have risen to prominence and the history of Scotland might have taken a different direction. As it was, with Thorfinn's help, MacBeth was accepted as High King and ruled well and wisely for seventeen years. It can be said that MacBeth's death in his prime, before the full effects of his years of peaceful and unified rule could be appreciated, was a great calamity for Scotland. Total unification was postponed for nearly two centuries and part of the country, Cumbria, was conquered by England later in the eleventh century. More importantly, Malcolm III, educated as he was in the English court, was instrumental in bringing about fundamental changes in the institutions of the kingdom, in the customs, laws and even the Church. The old Celtic order began to be displaced. MacBeth's death saw the beginning of the long, slow decline of Celtic Scotland, a decline that continues even to this day.

CHAPTER TEN

'By hereditary right, King of Scotland'
Charter of Duncan II

MacBeth has sometimes been described as the last Gaelic King of Scotland. Though this is not true it does underline the fact that the erosion of Gaelic Scotland began when Malcolm III was crowned at Scone on 25 April, 1058. To appreciate this point it is necessary to examine the struggle for succession in the half-century following MacBeth's death and the emergence of the great Scottish myth that Gaelic was always a minority language and culture in the country – the myth of the 'Highlander' and the 'Lowlander'.

Malcolm's actual name was Maol Cullum, the follower or servant of St Colm. To his Scottish subjects he became known as Maol Callum a' chinn mhòir, commonly anglicized to Malcolm Canmore, Malcolm the Bighead. This has been variously interpreted to mean 'the great head' or 'great leader'. However, it is more likely to refer to a physical aspect of Malcolm, as most Celtic names, especially nicknames, do.

Malcolm was not initially opposed to Gaelic; after all it was the language of the country, of the court, of administration, law, literature and religious worship. While the chroniclers state that it was his native tongue, Malcolm was proficient in other languages. From his Danish mother he would have learnt her language which was spoken by a substantial population in England including many highly placed nobles like Earl Siward. He was imbued with the Danish warrior's attitude that 'might is right'. At the court of Edward the Confessor, where he was brought up, he would have learnt Norman-French, Edward's own language, and learnt the concepts of Norman feudalism and attendant social attitudes. Lastly, he would have learnt the Anglo-Saxon tongue and the social concepts of that culture. When he claimed the throne of Scotland, his claim was not based on the complex Celtic laws of succession but on the alien concept of the unquestioned right of the oldest son to inherit his father's kingdom.

The Celtic system was already under great pressure from outside ideas and influences, mainly through the agency of the Christian Church. Certainly, concepts of primogeniture and private property were beginning to take root; nevertheless, when Malcolm III took power the Celtic system still prevailed. Perhaps, given the chance, it could have absorbed and adapted the new ideas into its own ethic. But the chance was not given. In all likelihood Malcolm Canmore became King against the will of the majority of the Scottish people. It had taken him more than three years to overthrow MacBeth and then Lulach, fighting strong Scottish opposition with a mercenary army mainly from Northumbria and including English, Danes and, in the last years, some Norman knights. After Malcolm's conquest of Scotland the leaders of his army were granted estates, especially in the Moray clan lands, by way of payment. For example *The Lamberton Charter* relates that 'Sir Robert de Lawdee got part lands in Moray for assisting Malcolm Canmore to recover the throne of Scotland'. These mercenaries who had fought for Malcolm were placed in powerful positions in Scotland and immediately introduced the feudal concepts of land tenure in the areas they settled.

It is significant that the province of Lothian was not returned to Northumbria as payment for its support of Malcolm. Perhaps this was due to Malcolm's territorial greed which became obvious later. In this area the former ruling and merchant class of Angles and Flemings seemed to return to their dominant position over the rural Celtic population and began to spread their influence further into Scotland.

The year 1066 was a fateful year for England's dynastic struggles and the events of that year not only brought important changes to England but were of significance to Scotland also. Edward the Confessor died on 5 January and Harold Godwinson, Edward's nominated heir, proclaimed himself king. But there were other claimants to the throne – the ambitious Duke William of Normandy, the ruthless Harald Hardrada, King of Norway, and the feckless Edgar Aetheling, son of Edward the Outlaw, who had been in exile in Hungary all his life. Edward the Outlaw, the son of Edmund Ironside, was of direct descent from the Anglo-Saxon kings of England and had been invited to return to the country by Edward the Confessor. He arrived in 1057 with his wife, Agatha, and his three children, Edgar, Margaret and Christina. Soon afterwards, perhaps by design, Edward the Outlaw was dead. When Harold Godwinson declared himself king, Edgar Aetheling did not challenge him. But challenges were to come immediately from Norway and Normandy.

In September, 1066, Harald Hardrada landed on the Yorkshire coast with an invading army. With him was Harold's brother, Tostig of Northumbria, still consumed with jealousy and hatred for his elder brother. Harold Godwinson met this force at Stamford Bridge on 25 September and defeated them. Among the dead were the King of Norway and Tostig. Hardly had Harold beaten the Norse army and sent the survivors fleeing back to their longboats when news reached him that William of Normandy had landed on the south coast. He force-marched his exhausted men down the country and met William at the field of Senlac near Hastings. Harold was slain in the battle on 14 October and England fell to William.

Edgar Aetheling now realized the danger of his own position. As the only surviving claimant to the English throne, it was obvious that if he remained in England William would have him killed. With his mother, Agatha, and his sisters, Margaret and Christina, he fled to Scotland and sought refuge with Malcolm Canmore. Malcolm not only gave the Aethelings sanctuary but he married Margaret. His first wife, Ingibjorg, died giving birth to her third son in 1067.

It is a myth of Scottish history that Margaret is supposed to have made the Scottish court speak English and so initiated the decline of Gaelic as the language of the Scottish ruling class. Margaret's father had lived all his life in Hungary and had married a Hungarian princess. It is specifically stated by some chroniclers that her brother Edgar was not seriously considered a suitable candidate for the English throne by the Witenagemot *because he could not speak English*. If that was so, it seems unlikely that his younger sister was fluent in the language.

It is certainly true that Margaret protested against the use of Gaelic in the churches in Scotland, where the mass was celebrated in the vulgar tongue, 'with I know not what barbaric rites'. Margaret instigated a debate on the state of the Scottish Church and invited three Benedictine monks from Canterbury to argue with the culdees and clergy on the merits of changing from Celtic to Roman usage. The result was that the Scottish Church was forced to fall in line with Rome and adopt Latin as the language of worship.

The primate of Scotland, Bishop Tuthald of St Andrews, had died in 1059 and was succeeded for a while by Bishop Fothudáin or Fothad. But Fothudáin was soon replaced by a Saxon named Turgot, Margaret's own confessor, who had accompanied her on her flight from England and who eventually wrote a biography of this formidable woman.

For her activities in forcing the Celtic Church in Scotland to fall in line with Rome, Margaret was canonized by a grateful church. She seems to have exercised considerable power over Malcolm Canmore and certainly possessed more of the qualities of Shakespeare's Lady Macbeth than Gruoch ever did. So great was her influence over Malcolm that he is reported to have solemnly kissed the books she read and stolen them from her chamber, returning them rebound in gold and jewels. He allowed her a totally free hand in the reorganization of the Scottish Church and court. She persuaded Malcolm to support her brother, Edgar Aetheling, in his claim to the English throne. She encouraged English refugees fleeing from the Norman conquerors to settle in Scotland, assuring them of positions of power and influence if they promised to support Edgar.

Four times Malcolm invaded England in an attempt to put Edgar on the throne, turning Northumbria into a slaughter house. Finally, in 1072, William the Conqueror led an army north and forced Malcolm to submit to him at Abernethy. Malcolm solemnly recognized William as his overlord and, in token of his future good behaviour, he surrendered his eldest son, Duncan, as a hostage to be brought up at the English court. But seven years later Malcolm's armies were again burning Northumbrian villages along the Tyne valley.

William the Conqueror died in 1087 and his son William Rufus now moved against Malcolm. He invaded Cumbria and annexed it as far as its capital, Caer Lliwelydd or Carlisle. That province was lost to Scotland from 1092 but Celtic was still spoken to some extent in Cumbria for another century or so. Place names, though anglicized, are still recognizable as Celtic, especially in the hill regions away from the fertile green valleys where the conquering English settlers built their homesteads.

Malcolm tried to come to terms with William Rufus and even journeyed to Gloucester, where the English King refused to see him. Angered by this rebuff, Malcolm returned to Scotland and once more invaded Northumbria. While leading an attack at Alnwick on 16 November, 1093, he was killed by a Norman knight named Morel of Bamborough. He was buried at Tynemouth but later his body was disinterred by his son, Alexander I, and buried at Dunfermline, the first Scottish King to break the tradition of burial on Iona. Edward, Malcolm's eldest son by Margaret, was also mortally wounded at Alnwick. He was carried to Jedburgh where he died. Three days after hearing the news from another of her sons, Edgar, who had also been at the battle, Margaret died. She too was buried at Dunfermline.

The people of Scotland saw in this turn of events an opportunity to rise up and rid the country of its alien rulers; to drive out the Norman and English settlers with their foreign concepts of land tenure and law. From the Hebrides came Malcolm's younger brother, sixty-year-old Domhnall Bàn (Fair Donald) whose name, as we have seen, is best remembered by a variety of anglicized spellings as Donald Ban, Donald Bane or, as in Shakespeare, Donalbain. Donald Ban appealed first and foremost to Scottish patriotism and, at the former capital of Scone (for Malcolm had moved the capital to Dùn Èideann, now called Edinburgh), he was elected High King of Scotland in the traditional manner. According to the *Anglo-Saxon Chronicle*, 'The Scots drove out all the English who were with King Malcolm before.' English and Norman alike were expelled and, along with them, the children of Malcolm and Margaret.

The return of an independent Gaelic Scotland was not a situation desired by William Rufus in spite of his differences with Malcolm and Margaret. William wanted to see Scotland ruled by a man who would acknowledge his overlordship of the country and dominated by Norman landowners and knights sympathetic to Norman rule in England. So he freed Duncan, Malcolm's eldest son by Ingibjorg, who had grown up as a Norman at the English court, and supplied him with an army of Norman and English knights. Duncan set off for Scotland, promising, if he succeeded in establishing himself as ruler, to recognize William Rufus as sovereign of all Britain. By May, 1094, Duncan's army had driven Donald Ban's clansmen across the Forth and Duncan had established himself in Edinburgh. He became the first Scottish King totally to reject the old Celtic system by styling himself 'I, Duncan, son of King Malcumb, *by hereditary right,* King of Scotia!'

Duncan did not rule for long. A few months later, on 12 November, 1094, he was slain by Maol Peadar Mac Leon, the Mormaer of the province of Cirech (Angus and Mearns). Donald Ban returned in triumph. He was helped by Edmund, one of Malcolm and Margaret's sons, whom he had allowed to return to Scotland and whom he appointed provincial ruler of southern Scotland under him. Donald Ban ruled Scotland for three years, during which time he attempted to return the country to its native customs, laws and methods of land tenure.

In October, 1097, Edgar, another of Malcolm and Margaret's sons, backed by an army once more supplied by William Rufus, invaded Scotland and managed to take Donald Ban prisoner. Edgar proclaimed himself king 'by hereditary right' and condemned his uncle to imprisonment and ordered that he should be deprived of his eyesight. His eyes were struck out while Edgar and his relatives looked on and it is said that Donald Ban, in his agony, seized the young son of his nephew, David (afterwards King of Scotland from 1124–53), and strangled him. Donald Ban eventually died at Roscobie in Forfar. He was buried at Dunkeld but loyal clansmen disinterred the body and reburied it on Iona. It was a symbolic gesture of defiance against the children of Malcolm and Margaret. As for Edmund, who had supported

Donald Ban, he was forced to become a monk and died in a monastery in Somerset.

With the ascendancy of the children of Malcolm and Margaret – Edgar, Alexander and David succeeding each other to the throne – the end of Celtic laws and customs was only a matter of time. All these rulers were brought up in an Anglo-Norman environment and they encouraged the settlement of an Anglo-Norman ruling class in Scotland. So it is feasible to say that in MacBeth Scotland had its last great Gaelic ruler. He represented the native order as opposed to the foreign feudal order which began with the coming of Malcolm Canmore to the throne.

From this time onwards the language of the ruling class in Scotland was first Norman-French and then English. Because of this the language of the Scottish people eventually changed so that at the last count only 88,415 (1971 Census) Scotsmen and women spoke Scottish Gaelic as their first language. But a myth has been created in Scotland that Gaelic never was the universal language of the country. The myth is commonly referred to as the 'Highland' and 'Lowland' myth. It proposes that Scotland always contained two distinct nationalities – Highlanders who were Gaelic in speech and Lowlanders who had always been Teutonic or English in speech. Even today Scottish history books are published with maps of Scotland showing a 'Highland/Lowland' line separating the two 'nationalities'.

Many times over the centuries historians have attacked this popularly held belief – but with scant success. Centuries of brainwashing are hard to erase. In *The Scottish War of Independence: A Critical Study*, 1914, Evan MacLeod Barron wrote:

> It is high time, indeed, that the English myth in Scotland was exploded once and for all. The only people of English blood who are found in any numbers in Scotland are the people of Lothian ... Moreover, all recent research goes to show that in the thirteenth century the language of the bulk of the people outside Lothian was Celtic. In the districts to the south of the Forth and Clyde as well as to the north, Celtic, save in Lothian, was the popular tongue.

In the same year, Professor W. J. Watson, in 'The Position of Gaelic in Scotland' (his inaugural address at Edinburgh

University) stated that 'Gaelic attained its greatest extent in the eleventh century when at the time of Carham in 1018 it ran from Tweed and Solway to Pentland Firth'. But in spite of such excellent works as Watson's *History of the Celtic Place Names of Scotland* (Blackwood, 1926), the 'Highland/Lowland' myth is still current in Scotland.

In order to stress the significance for Scotland, linguistically and culturally, of MacBeth's overthrow, it is necessary to make what might at first glance appear to be a digression from this study and to examine very briefly the evidence that Gaelic was the universal tongue in Scotland. This digression is necessary in view of the intransigence of those who still believe in the 'two nations' myth. It will also become clear why there is such a lack of written documentation in Gaelic in Scotland. The persecution of Gaelic, especially during the years of the Reformation in Scotland, saw the destruction of whole libraries of Gaelic literature.

The evidence indicates that it took many centuries to push Gaelic back into the 'Highlands', that Gaelic became current in the Lothian territory annexed by Malcolm II from Northumbria, that Gaelic was even used across the border in Northumbria. It will be remembered that the basic population in this Lothian area (not to be confused with the modern Lothian counties) was Brythonic Celtic and that the ruling class were Angle and Fleming settlers. All over this 'Lowland' area of southern Scotland, Gaelic place names are found in such profusion that it is obvious they were not given by invading skirmishers but by generations of Gaelic-speaking inhabitants. Take Peebles, for example, where there are ninety-nine pure Gaelic place names such as Fingland from *Fhionn Ghleann*, the bright glen; Achinghall from *Achadh nan Gall*, the field of the strangers; and Kilduff, south-east of Edinburgh, from *Coille Dubh*, the black wood. Dalry, now part of the city of Edinburgh, could come from *Dail an Righ*, king's meadow, or *Dail Fhraoigh*, heather meadow. Gilmerton, near Edinburgh, comes from *Gille Mhuire*, Mary's servant. The Braid Hills are named from *Braghaid*, a dative of *Braighe*, meaning upper park. Glencourse, written Glencrosk in the fourteenth century, means 'glen of the crossings' or *Gleann Crosg*. In confirmation, there are three different old crossings in the area.

Drumsheugh (written Drumselch in 1507) comes from *Drum Seileach* or willow ridge; Currie is taken from the dative of *Curach* – a wet place. Craighentinnie comes from *Creag an tSionneaigh* – the fox's rock. Close to Castellan of Dunbar is a knoll called Knockenhair from *Cnoc an h-Aire*, the watch hill. One could go on indefinitely wandering through the 'Lowlands' deciphering Gaelic names but these few examples should be sufficient.

Galloway, in south-west Scotland, remained Gaelic in speech until the eighteenth century. Towards the end of the fifteenth century two notable poets clashed in literary battle. One of them was Walter Kennedy, son of Gilbert, Lord Kennedy of Carrick, a Gaelic poet, and the other was William Dunbar who represented the new 'Inglis' speaking order in Scotland. In a long poem, *The Flyting, or Scalding, of Dunbar and Kennedy*, Dunbar accuses Kennedy (c. 1460–1508) of being too Gaelic and contrasts the characteristics of the Gaels with those of the 'Inglis' speakers to whom he belongs. Kennedy, who was born and raised in Dunure, Ayrshire, condemns Dunbar's superior attitudes and answers that Gaelic was the only language for anyone who called himself a Scotsman. 'It was the good language of this land,' he said, 'and caused Scotland to multiply and spread.'

An English official preparing a report between 1563–66 on the possibility of the military occupation of Carrick, Kyle and Cunningham by an English army wrote of the town of Carrick: 'The people for the moste parte spekeht Erische.' *Galloway Gossip*, 1901, quotes a report that as late as 1762 the parish of Barr in Carrick had advertised for a schoolmaster and it was particularly requested 'that he budst be able tae speak Gaelic (and) the man they took was frae aboot the Lennox.' The same records show that during the 1715 and 1745 insurrections in Scotland, Highland troops passed through the area. 'Forbye whun the Rebels wus passin' through Gallowa' and Carrick in 1715 and 1745 the Hielanmen wus able tae converse freely with the natives, but naither the natives nor the Hielanmen could talk wi' the Erisch auxiliaries for their Gaelic wus that different they cud hardly mak them oot.' Margaret MacMurray of Cultzeon, near Maybole, who died about 1760, was generally accredited with having been the last native speaker of Gaelic in Carrick. And be it remembered that Robert Burns was born near Ayr 'upon the Carrick border' in 1759.

In 1725 the English traveller Edward Burt, writing in *Letters from a Gentleman in the North of Scotland*, observed that Gaelic was current in Fife, just opposite Edinburgh, until the early eighteenth century. He says that until the Union of 1707 it was made a condition that when a boy or girl was bound as an apprentice on the Edinburgh side of the Forth, he or she had to be taught English. Burt also says that Sir James Foulis of Colington had informed him 'he had it from an old man, who spoke Gaelic, that even in his time it was almost the *universal* language of Fife'.

According to Andrew Trevisano, the Venetian ambassador, writing about 1500:

> The language of the Scots is the same as that of the Irish, and very different from the English; but many of the Scottish people speak English extremely well, in consequence of the intercourse they have with each other on the borders.

Hector Boece, writing about 1527, and probably more responsible than any man for the Macbeth of Shakespeare's vision, admitted that 'those of us who live on the borders of England have foresaken our mother tongue (Gaelic) and learned English being driven thereto by wars and commerce'.

Another historian of the time, John Major, in *The History of Greater Britain*, 1521, also admitted that the majority of Scots had spoken Gaelic only 'a short time ago' and that the language was still in fairly widespread use. This is also confirmed by the historian George Buchanan who mentions the widespread use of Gaelic in southern Scotland during the sixteenth century.

Blind Harry, a Scottish Poet, presents us with evidence that the redoubtable William Wallace, who became Guardian of Scotland during the Second Interregnum in 1296–1306, spoke Gaelic. In his work on Wallace, Blind Harry has an English soldier sneering at Wallace in Gaelic:

> Sen ye are Scots, yeit salust sall ye be
> Gud Deyn, *Deagh* Lord,
> *Bach laoch, bennachd a de.*

In other words: 'Since you are a Scotsman, I shall salute you thus,' and he goes off into a piece of Gaelic nonsense which he has obviously picked up: 'good faith, good Lord, young boy hero, blessings of God'. He clearly wanted to show off his knowledge. Harry confirms that Wallace spoke Gaelic or 'Ersche', as he called it, by emphasizing that Wallace had an 'Ersche mantill'.

Robert the Bruce is on record as holding a parliament at St Modan's Priory, Ardchattan, in 1308, which conducted its business in Gaelic. James IV (1488–1513) is noted by the Spanish Ambassador to his court, Señor Ayala, to have spoken Gaelic. James IV seems to have been the last Scottish monarch able to speak the language.

By the early fifteenth century a change in linguistic thinking had taken place in Scotland. Previously, John of Fordun was quite clear in saying that the language spoken by the ruling class and merchants was English or 'Inglis' and that Gaelic, spoken by the majority of the people, was 'Scottish'. But to tell the English-speaking Scots, having fought for the independence of their country under Wallace and Bruce, that they were speaking the language of the enemy would not do. So that they could retain their Scottish nationality without becoming Scottish in speech, the anglicized Scots and descendants of the Norman and English settlers, started to call the Scottish language Yrisch, Ersch and Irish (and today, Gaelic) with the inference that it was something non-Scottish. Their own English speech then became Scots, Scottish or sometimes 'Lallans' (Lowlands). Gavin Douglas (1457–1522) was the first writer to call the Scottish dialect of English 'Scots'. Thus another wedge was driven between the Gaelic-speaking Scot and the anglicized Scot; another prop for the 'Highland/Lowland' myth.

A further blow, about the same time, was the Scottish Reformation, which has been described as an achievement of English foreign policy. Certainly, whatever lay behind the Reformation, there arose in Scotland an anti-Gaelic government dedicated to the total extirpation of Gaelic. The Kirk saw Gaelic as an obstacle to the spread of Protestant ideas and created institutions which were described as 'English schools for rooting out the Irish language and other pious uses'. These institutions, still strangely looked upon as a progressive educational system by modern Scottish historians, were merely the instruments of a sustained policy of cultural genocide in Scotland.

The Reformation can be blamed for the lack of old literature in the Scottish Gaelic language. James Loch, an architect of the nineteenth-century genocidal 'clearances', tried to justify his policy of stamping out the language by saying that nothing had ever been written in Gaelic and therefore it was a worthless language. Even today responsible historians like George Pryde seem to propagate this weird theory. But there are remains; and such Gaelic literature that has come down to us, meagre evidence though it may be, shows that the Scottish Gaels were heirs to an extremely ancient and sophisticated culture which fell on evil days after the death of MacBeth.

We must remember that Irish, Manx and Scottish Gaelic developed as dialects of a common Goidelic Celtic tongue and that the divergence only began about the fourth century. Irish literature, with its sophisticated mythology, was the third written European language after Greek and Latin and contains Europe's oldest vernacular literature. At the time Irish was first committed to a written form it was substantially the same language as Scottish Gaelic. Therefore it is possible to claim that Scottish Gaelic was equally the heir to that literature.

Libraries full of Gaelic works must have been destroyed by the anti-Gaelic administrators of the country. One such complete library of Gaelic books was seen and catalogued by the Celtic scholar Edward Lhuyd in 1699; the catalogue survived but the library was destroyed. It is sad to reflect on the wealth of literature which must have perished. But all that is left is *The Book of Deer* with its Gaelic notations from the ninth century, and one eleventh century poem. There is a surprising gap before we find the Islay Charter of 1408 (witnessed coincidentally by one Fergus MacBeth). This charter not only demonstrates a sophisticated literary medium, the obvious product of a long tradition of writing in the language, but also proves that Gaelic was still being used as the language of administration, for which it was absolutely necessary.

From the purely literary viewpoint the most important surviving manuscript is the *Book of the Dean of Lismore*, compiled between 1512 and 1526. It contains an anthology of Gaelic poetry. The first known Gaelic printed book was Bishop John Carswell's *Form na h-Òrdaigh*, 1567, a prayer book which translated John Knox's liturgy. And yet such is the disrepute in which Gaelic is now held that as recently as 1961 a Scottish historian, George Pryde, in *A New History of Scotland*, could solemnly assure his readers that the first book was not printed in Gaelic until the late eighteenth century, in spite of the fact that the entire Bible was published in Gaelic in 1690.

Dr I. F. Grant, in the *History of the Clan MacLeod*, asks the significant question, 'There are no rent rolls, deeds of fosterage or similar documents as early as Rory Mór [Rory Mór MacLeod of Dunvegan, d. 1626]. Can it have been that they were all destroyed?' The simple answer is yes. The destruction was almost complete; but, pathetic though the remnants are, they are evidence of a wealth of literature and records in Gaelic which was destroyed.

The linguistic change has had a profound effect on the country's understanding of its past. This destruction of records, this lack of knowledge of the customs and culture of eleventh century Scotland, indeed, the lack of knowledge of the very language spoken by the people of Scotland at that time, made it possible for MacBeth to be transformed from one of the more progressive rulers in Scottish history into a murderous petty kinglet.

CHAPTER ELEVEN

'This dead butcher and his fiend-like queen'
Macbeth, Act V Scene 7

So great are the differences between the personality and behaviour of the MacBeth of history and the Macbeth of Shakespeare's play that it is a natural question to ask whether the latter was not purely the creation of Shakespeare's artistic fantasy. Was Macbeth conjured into being, alone and unaided, by the playwright for the sake of his art or, as some have darkly suggested, as a piece of political hack writing to please his new monarch, James VI of Scotland, newly acclaimed James I of England?

If Shakespeare's Macbeth is false to the real MacBeth, it is not because Shakespeare wished or even knew it to be so. In writing his play he used the best sources available in the English language in the London of his day. The degeneration of MacBeth of Scotland into a murdering usurper began some 350 years after his death at Lumphanan. As has been emphasized, the histories were written from an English cultural viewpoint, albeit by anglicized Scotsmen. The historians were almost totally removed, linguistically and culturally, from the eleventh century Scotland about which they were writing. They were unable to check contemporary sources, appeared to have had no knowledge of the language, could not examine the Celtic laws which operated at the time and were brought up under feudal laws and concepts. The dangers of making pronouncements on systems based on different cultural concepts is clearly demonstrated by a nineteenth-century historian, Professor A. J. Church, who could seriously remark that the struggle for kingship in Scotland was a remarkably bloodthirsty business *for hardly ever did a son succeed his father to the throne*! It is a sad reflection of the cultural divide between Gaelic Scotland and its modern progeny, English Scotland. It is this divide that was responsible for the creation of Shakespeare's Macbeth.

John of Fordun, the Canon of Aberdeen, writing in 1384, first turns MacBeth into a usurper and an oppressor of the Scottish people. And, as we have seen, he was the first to mention Macduff, supposedly exiled for his friendship with Duncan's sons. Macduff is certainly a common enough Gaelic name, *Mac Dubh* – son of the black man. But there is no contemporary evidence for Macduff and certainly Fordun does not mention the murder of his wife or children. Nor does he make any mention of Banquo. He does, however, make one very deliberate change. When he discovers that Duncan's father was Crinan, Abbot of Dunkeld, he alters the reference because he is unable to accept that churchmen, not only in the Celtic Church but in the Roman Church of the eleventh century, were not celibate. Priests in Fordun's day were forbidden to marry, so he totally dismissed the possibility of Duncan's father being an abbot. Interestingly, at the end of his account, Fordun comments bitterly that an historian named William (of Malmesbury?) gives all praise to Siward for MacBeth's overthrow and none to Malcolm.

Not long after Fordun wrote his history, Andrew of Wyntoun, the Prior of St Serf's at Loch Leven in Fife, also wrote a history (c. 1395–1424). Wyntoun does not interfere with the name and title of Duncan's father and clearly records him as Crinan, Abbot of Dunkeld. However, he then proceeds to make MacBeth the son of Duncan's sister, and MacBeth's wife, Gruoch, the widow of Duncan instead of the widow of Gillecomgain. Wynton makes no mention of Banquo but does say that Macduff was forced to flee to Fife because of his friendship with Duncan's sons. He does not have MacBeth kill Macduff's wife and children. Wyntoun's own contribution to the myth of MacBeth is the invention of the story of the three weird sisters who foretell the rise and fall of the Scottish monarch. Even so, Wyntoun was still close enough to original sources to admit:

This MacBeth did many pleasand actis in the begynning of his regnne under culour of justice but att last he schew his crewlte and pervest mynd, sett to shedding of blude mair then ony zeile or justice. ...

But while Fordun called MacBeth a usurper, it is Wyntoun who first records Duncan's death as murder.

It is Hector Boece, the friend and fellow student of Erasmus and first principle of Aberdeen University, founded in 1496, who is the real originator of the Macbeth of Shakespeare's vision. Hector Boece wrote his history of Scotland in Latin and published it in Paris in 1527. Lord Hals later commented on Boece's bias that 'the Scots have been reformed from Popery but not from Hector Boece'.

Boece invented the character of Banquo as the progenitor of the line of Stewart kings; he turned Duncan's death into a poisoning; he invented the murder of Lady Macduff and her children; he amplified the role of the three weird sisters; and, finally, it was Boece who turned Gruoch into Lady MacBeth and laid the foundation for one of the most evil women in literature. Boece writes:

> His wife, impatient of lang tarry (as all women ar) specially quhar they are desirus of any purpos, gaif him gret artation to pusew the weird that sche might be ane queene, calland him off tymis febye cowart and nocht desirus of honouris, sen he durst not assailze the thing with manheid and curage quilk is offerit to hym be the benivolence of fortoun. Howbeat sindry otheris hes assalzeit sich things afore with mast terribyl jeopardyis quhen they had not sic sickerness to succeid in the end of them laboris as he had.

Boece's original version in Latin became extremely popular. We find, as early as 1546, John Bellinden, Archdeacon of Moray, translating it into English for the use of James V. And William Stewart made a translation into verse for the young King between 1531 and 1535. Boece's version of the MacBeth story became the standard work on the subject. Even George Buchanan (1506–1582), whose *History of Scotland* is one of the most learned and critical works, failed to correct the errors of his predecessor.

Contemporary with Buchanan was the English historian, Ralph Holinshed, about whom little is known except that he died in 1580. Holinshed wrote *The Chronicles of England, Scotland and Ireland*, which began publication in London in 1577. It is now generally accepted that it was to Holinshed's *Chronicle* that Shakespeare turned for background material for his drama. And Holinshed's history was taken from the story which had been invented by Boece, although even Holinshed made the concession that

> Macbeth (was) a valiant gentleman, and one that if he had not been somewhat cruel of nature, might have been thought most worthy of government of a realm.

Having established how the historical figure of MacBeth had become distorted by the sixteenth century, we can now ask what made Shakespeare choose this particular subject for a play? The principal reason for choosing a play with a Scottish theme was the union of the crowns of Scotland and England in the person of James Stewart. The Stewarts could trace their ancestry back to Robert II (1371–90) who was the son of Marjorie, a daughter of Robert Bruce, and Walter, High Steward of Scotland. The line went further back, according to the Stewarts, directly to Malcolm Canmore. They were hardly likely, therefore, to appreciate a flattering portrayal of the man their ancestor had overthrown. Boece's invention of Banquo as the founder of the Stewart line was probably an effort to win Stewart patronage, which certainly worked in his case. In using the mythical character of Banquo, Shakespeare, too, won the appreciation of the King.

James VI, who was born in Edinburgh on 19 July, 1566, was barely a year old when he was crowned King of Scotland. He considered himself something of a scholar and wrote such works as a *Counterblast to Tobacco* and a work on witchcraft called *Daemonologie*, written when he was twenty-five years old. When in March, 1603, Elizabeth I of England died, the succession was offered to James who was crowned on 7 May, 1603 as James I of England. As early as May, 1604, James had confirmed a royal licence for the Globe Theatre. Shakespeare's plays were very popular at James's court and William Oldys related that James once wrote to Shakespeare 'in his own hand'. During December, 1603, the Globe company performed at Wilton where James was paying a visit to William Herbert, the third Earl of Pembroke. In

March, 1604, the company walked in procession, accompanying the King into London. In August that year they were at Somerset House where James was greeting the new Spanish ambassador, Juan de Taxis, Conde de Villa Medina.

Under this new patronage, Shakespeare's activity increased and he turned his talent to producing a play in the King's honour. But James was a difficult audience to write for. He easily became restless and impatient. One evening, while visiting Oxford, he became bored by a Greek play translated into Latin and performed for his benefit. It is recorded that he 'spoke many words of dislike'. The next evening, during a comedy, James 'distasted it and fell asleep, and when he wakened he would have been gone, saying "I marvel what they think me to be".'

A suitable subject had to be chosen that would pander to the King's interests: some degree of witchcraft would have to be introduced, as well as his ancestry, and, above all, the play would have to make reference to the beneficial aspects of the union of Scotland and England.

The story of MacBeth was an easy choice for it had been a popular topic in Elizabethan London. It had already been the subject of various poems and plays. A *Ballad of Macdobeth* was registered copyright with the Stationers' Company on 27 August, 1596. It was the same ballad that a Thomas Millyngton was fined eleven shillings and six pence for printing 'contrary to order, which he also presently paid. And the ballad entitled *The Taming of the Shrew* also one other *Ballad of Macdobeth*'. Thomas Kempe in his *Nine Dais Wonder* (1600) makes an allusion to a 'penny poet' who wrote 'the miserable stolen story of Macdoel or Macdobeth or Mac something, for I am sure a Mac it was, though I never had the maw to see it.' In April, 1602, the Earl of Nottingham's actors were preparing to stage a play on the same theme entitled *Malcolm, King of Scottes*, while it is also possible that MacBeth was the subject of a comic play in London at an earlier date which caused the English ambassador to Scotland, George Nicholson, to write to Lord Burleigh on 15 April, 1598:

It is regretted that comedians of London should scorn the King and people of the land in this play and it is wished that the matter be speedily amended lest the King and the country be striven to answer.

To Shakespeare MacBeth seemed an ideal subject and all he had to do was turn to Holinshed, perhaps even to Boece, to find all the ingredients he needed.

It is generally supposed that *Macbeth* had its first performance before James I and his royal guest, King Christian IV of Denmark, during the Danish King's visit to England between 17 July and 11 August, 1606. It seems more likely that the first performance took place at Hampton Court on 7 August, one of three occasions when Shakespeare's company acted before the King. The play was not registered with the Stationers' Company until 8 November, 1623, when it was printed in a volume of collected works.

Right from the opening moment, with the simple stage direction 'Thunder and lightning. Enter three witches.' the attention of James VI was held rapt.

First Witch. When shall we three meet again
In thunder, lightning, or in rain?
Second Witch. When the hurlyburly's done,
When the battle's lost and won.
Third Witch. That will be ere the set of sun.
First Witch. Where the place?
Second Witch.   Upon the heath.
Third Witch. There to meet with Macbeth.

Shakespeare knew the interest that James had in the myth of the three witches who foretold not only Macbeth's rise and fall but also told the mythical Banquo that he would beget a line of kings though he would not be one himself. The year before the first performance of *Macbeth*, Doctor Matthew Gwinn, a Fellow of St John's College, Oxford, had organized a play called *Three Sybils* concerning the myth of Banquo and the three witches. In this dramatization the three Sybils hail Banquo first as King of Scotland, secondly as King of England and thirdly as King of Ireland. Gwinn actually made the Sybils into 'goddesses, nymphs or fairies', which was the description given by both Boece and Holinshed. In repeating this motif, Shakespeare turned the three Sybils into three traditional Scottish witches with withered skins, beards and other physical deformities.

Whatever Shakespeare's motivation in writing the play,

artistically it is an immortal classic about the anatomy of evil. G. K. Hunter, introducing a Penguin Books edition of the play in 1967, stated that 'reduced to its plot-line *Macbeth* sounds like a crime-does-not-pay melodrama'. But *Macbeth* is more concerned with the uncovering of the criminal to himself; of all Shakespeare's plays *Macbeth* is the one most obsessively concerned with evil. Hunter says:

> Here the evil is, for once and without doubt, larger, more fascinating, more effective than the pallid representation of good (Act III, Scene 2):
>
> > Good things of day begin to droop and drowse,
> > Whiles night's black agents to their preys do rouse.

Certainly 'night's black agents' stalk Macbeth. And when he falls – the triumph of good over evil – he falls because his tyranny produces the engines of its own destruction. 'The movement that carries Malcolm, Macduff and Siward above him is generated first by his own downward tendency,' says Hunter, 'and only secondarily by their efforts.'

In Lady MacBeth, Shakespeare has created the immortal evil wife, but, although she is evil, she is represented basically as an accomplice rather than an instigator. Her function is to push Macbeth *after* he has accepted the 'suggestion' of the three witches. She keeps him to the course he has already set. She asks (Act I, Scene 7):

> Art thou afeard
> To be the same in thine own act and valour

Shakespeare presents Macbeth as a man primarily spurred on by his own ambitions. Macbeth himself admits (Act I, Scene 7):

> I have no spur
> To prick the sides of my intent, but only
> Vaulting ambition, which o'er-leaps itself
> And falls on the other

Shakespeare follows Holinshed and Boece in making Lady Macbeth the nurturing and driving force of Macbeth's ambition, turning that ambition into a positive line of action. Holinshed wrote:

The words of the three weird sisters also greatly encouraged him, but specially his wife lay sore upon him to attempt the thing as she was very ambitious, breathing in unquenchable desire to bear the name of a queen.

Shakespeare's pen translated the Lady Macbeth of Holinshed and Boece from merely an ambitious, scheming woman into something almost fiendish in quality. Nothing is surely more horrific than Lady MacBeth's statement (Act I, Scene 7):

> I have given suck, and know
> How tender 'tis to love the babe that milks me;
> I would, while it was smiling in my face
> Have plucked my nipple from his boneless gums
> And dashed the brains out, had I so sworn as you
> Have done to this.

There is no denying the greatness of Shakespeare's creation. As a work of art it is churlish to say that historical research denies the veracity of this or that point in the play. In this respect the poet exercises an artist's freedom in selecting, modifying and inventing without regard to historical accuracy. John MacBeth has written:

> The name Shakespeare is sacrosanct as the ideal artist and supreme poet of England. But it can do no good to concede as privilege to genius what one feels to be wrong – it was not only for artistic creation but to please his royal patron (that Shakespeare) loaded Macbeth with volcanic and satanic passions bordering on the inhuman and mentally deranged.

We must concede that if Shakespeare's Macbeth is confused with MacBeth, the High King of Scotland, then John MacBeth does have a point. The valuations which Shakespeare wrote into his plays were, naturally enough, the Elizabethan Englishman's valuations of Scotland with all their inborn prejudices. The voice of comment is Scottish when Malcolm and Macduff meet to discuss the situation in Scotland before the King's Palace in England, but the words are those of an Englishman. The bias is obvious. Scotland is 'a poor country' in a state 'where violent sorrow seems a modern ecstasy', while England is always gracious England' and Duncan is 'a most sacred King'. But it would be foolish to hold Shakespeare so sacrosanct as to deny him human failings and prejudices.

The setting of Shakespeare's play is somewhat of an irrelevancy. It was certainly not set in eleventh century Scotland, no more than it was set in the Scotland of Shakespeare's time. It has an almost 'never-never-world' quality to it, demonstrated by the fact that the story has been acceptably translated to medieval Japan in *Throne of Blood*, a film made in 1957, and to the Chicago of the 1920's in the film *Joe Macbeth*, made in 1955.

From the historical viewpoint it is unfortunate that MacBeth has come down to us in the Shakespearian image of 'this dead butcher and his fiend-like queen'. But even had Shakespeare never written the play, this image was the one projected by historians such as Boece. For good or ill the character of Macbeth had been firmly established throughout the world. Let us hope that we can now clearly differentiate between the Macbeth of fiction and the MacBeth of historical reality, so that when we speak of the High King of Scotland we will no longer dismiss him with Young Siward's words (Act V, Scene 7):

> The devil himself could not pronounce a title
> More hateful to mine ear.

Rather it will be St Berchan's summary on the reign of MacBeth which we can now apply to that much maligned Scottish monarch:

> The strong one was fair, yellow haired and tall.
> Very pleasant was the handsome youth to me.
> Brimful of food was Scotland, east and west,
> During the reign of the ruddy, brave king.

SELECT BIBLIOGRAPHY

Sources are quoted where deemed necessary in the text. The following works are merely a selection of the major source material used in this work and is in no way meant to be a comprehensive list.

Early sources:

Anglo-Saxon Chronicle. ed. Dorothy Whitelock, Eyre & Spottiswoode, London, 1961.

Annals of Loch Cé. ed. W. M. Hennessy. Dublin, 1871.

Annals of Ulster (431–1540 AD*).* ed. B. MacCarthy, Dublin, 1887–95.

Florence of Worcester. *Chronicon ex Chronicis.* ed. B. Thorpe. London, 1848/49.

Marianus Scotus. *Chronicon.* ed. G. Wütz. 1844.

Orkneyinga Saga. ed. Alexander Burt Taylor. Oliver & Boyd, Edinburgh, 1938.

Prioratus Sancti Andree in Scotia. Bannatyne Club, 1841.

Prophecy of St. Berchan. MS 23/G4 Royal Irish Academy, Dublin.

Symeon of Durham. *Historia Dunelmensis Eclesiae.* trs. ed. J. Stevenson, 1855.

Secondary sources: (chronological order)

De Fordun: John de Fordun. *Chronica Gentis Scotorum* (circa 1380) ed. W. F. Skene, Edinburgh, 1871/2.

Wyntoun: Andrew of Wyntoun. *The Orygynale Cronykil of Scotland.* ed. David Ley, Edinburgh, 1879.
Boece: Hector Boece. *Historia de Scotia*, Paris, 1527.
Holinshed: Ralph Holinshed. *Chronicles of England, Scotland and Ireland*, London, 3 volumes, 1577.
Buchanan: *George Buchanan's History of Scotland*, 1583.

General works:

Anderson, Alan Orr. *Early Sources of Scottish History 500 AD to 1286 AD.* Oliver & Boyd, Edinburgh, 1922.
Dunbar, Sir Archibald. *Scottish Kings: A Revised Chronology of Scottish History 1005–1625.* David Douglas, Edinburgh, 1899.
Duncan, Archibald A. M. *Scotland – The Making of a Kingdom.* Oliver & Boyd, Edinburgh, 1975.
Erskine, Hon. Stuart R. J. *MacBeth: being an historical figure.* Robert Carruthers, Inverness, 1930.
Ferguson, Sir James. *The Man Behind Macbeth*, Faber & Faber, London, 1969.
Hume, Dr. Abraham. *Who Was Macbeth?* Liverpool Mercury Reprint, 1853.
Hutton, Clayton. *Macbeth: The Making of the Film.* Max Parrish, London, 1960.
MacAuliffe, M. J. *Gaelic Law*, 1924.
MacBeth, John. *MacBeth, King, Queen & Clan.* W. J. Hay, Edinburgh, 1921.
MacKinnon, Kenneth. *The Lion's Tongue.* Club Leabhar, Inverness, 1974.
Mann, H. K. *The Lives of the Popes in the Middle Ages: the Popes of the Gregorian renaissance St. Leo IX to Honorious II, 1049–1130.* Kegan Paul, Trench & Trubner, 1910.
Russell, Edward R. (Lord Russell of Liverpool). *The True Macbeth.* Literary & Philosophical Society of Liverpool Reprint, 1875.
Shakespeare, William. *Macbeth*, with the history of Macbeth from Ralph Holinshed's Chronicle of Scotland, 1577. Cassells, 1884.
Shakespeare, William. *Macbeth*, ed. G. K. Hunter. Penguin Books, 1967.

125

Skene, William F. *Celtic Scotland*. 3 vols. David Douglas, Edinburgh, 1886.

Stevens, Professor George. *Macbeth, Earl Siward and Dundee:* a contribution to Scottish history from the Rune finds of Scandinavia. Edinburgh, 1876.

Stopes, Mrs M. *The Scottish and English Macbeth*. Pamphlet, 1897.

Walker, Reginald F. *Companion to the study of Shakespeare's Macbeth*, 1947.

Watson, William J. *The History of the Celtic Place Names of Scotland*. William Blackwood, Edinburgh, 1926.

GLOSSARY OF PERSONAL NAMES

Some of the Celtic personal names of eleventh century Scotland and their meaning: Because of the 'language break' the names of Celtic Scotland have mostly been written down through English phonetics. The following is a selected list of some of the prominent personal names mentioned in MacBeth's story, with their original spelling and (where possible) meaning.

Anglicization	Gaelic	Meaning
Angus	Aonghas	Ancient name thought to be 'a choice'
Bethoc	Beathag	Early saint's name.
Columba	Colm or Callum	Irish saint who brought Christianity to Scotland.
Donald	Domhnall	World chief.
Duncan	Donnchadh	Brown warrior.
Dungal	Dumngual	Gaelicized Strathclyde British name.
Fothad	Fothudáin	Ancient name used by one of three leaders of the Fianna who took possession of Scotland in the third century.
Finlay	Findlaech	
Gillecomgain	Gille-Chomgain	Servant of St. Comgain.

Girc	Girc	Early saint found as Maol Girc, Abbot of Fore in *Book of Deer*.
Gospatrick	Gwas-Padruig	Strathclyde British name, Servant of St. Patrick.
Kenneth	Coinneach	Handsome.
Macbeth	Mac Bheatha	Son of Life.
Madach	Maddach	Strathclyde British name.
Malcolm	Maol Callum	Follower of St. Columba.
Melmore	Maol Mhuire	Follower of Mary.
Melsnecti	Maol Snechta	Follower of Snow.
Rory	Ruaidhri	Red or foxy headed.

INDEX

129